D0568224

A Taste of Tradition

A Taste of Tradition

A Culinary Collection

OPRYLAND HOTEL

Published by Opryland Hotel

Copyright© Opryland Hotel
A Gaylord Entertainment℠ Company
2800 Opryland Drive
Nashville, Tennessee 37214
615-889-1000

Jack Vaughn *President, Opryland Hospitality and Attractions*
Joe Henry *Vice-President, Hospitality*
Ray Waters *Hotel Manager*

Shirlee Lawrence-Verploegen *Manager/Buyer, Retail*
Donnie Beauchamp *Photography*
Richard Gerst *Culinary Collection*

Karen Groom *Director, Marketing Services*
Kathy Demonbreun *Manager, Marketing Services*

Tom Adkinson *Manager, Media Relations*
Judy Mizell *Manager, Public Relations*

All rights reserved. No part of this publication may be reproduced in any form or by any means, electronic or mechanical, including photocopy and information storage and retrieval systems, without permission in writing from the publisher.

Edited, Designed and Manufactured by
Favorite Recipes® Press
an imprint of

FRP

P.O. Box 305142
Nashville, Tennessee 37230
1-800-358-0560

Mary Cummings *Managing Editor*
Jane Hinshaw *Project Manager*
Bruce Gore *Book Design*
Steve Newman *Art Director*
Mark Sloan *Production Manager*

ISBN Number: 0-9654699-0-5
Library of Congress Number: 96-092744
First Printing: 1996
Second Printing: 1997

This cookbook
is dedicated to the memory of

Roy Acuff and Minnie Pearl

The King of Country Music
ROY ACUFF

and

The Queen of Country Comedy
MINNIE PEARL

brightened the lives of millions for more than 50 years
every time they held court on stage at the Grand Ole Opry.
Mr. Roy and Miss Minnie were mainstays at the Opry during its
formative years on WSM Radio. He joined in 1938 and she two
years later in 1940. Both contributed greatly to the international
success of this radio show which, in turn, spawned the vast
Opryland USA complex, beginning in the early 1970s.

This royal couple entertained regularly at the
Opry during those years and watched and participated
in the development of the Opryland Themepark in the early 1970s,
the relocation of the Grand Ole Opry to the new Opry House in 1974
and the opening of the spectacular Opryland Hotel at Opryland USA
in 1977. They continued to bring love and laughter to country music
fans via TNN: The Nashville Network before their deaths—
his in 1992 and hers in 1996.

In tribute to their many contributions to
the entertainment world and to Opryland USA, these
two Country Music Hall of Fame members are prominently
featured in the magnificent brick mural that greets guests as they
drive into the Opryland Hotel's Cascades Lobby motor entrance.
The likenesses of these two Grand Ole Opry greats in this mural
serve as a reminder that Roy Acuff and Minnie Pearl were—
and are still today—an integral part of the
Opryland Hotel's grand tradition.

Contents

Foreword

Millions of guests annually stay at or visit the Opryland Hotel in Nashville, Tennessee. Many are here for business meetings or conventions, while others are drawn to this world-famous hotel and convention center because they have seen or heard about it on television or by word of mouth from friends and relatives.

In the course of my work with the hotel, I witness many of our guests as they walk through the halls, lobbies, and indoor gardens, marveling at the beautiful facilities. So many of them come into our retail shops asking questions about the hotel and looking for just the right souvenir to take home to help them remember this magnificent property.

A frequent request from our guests is for a book describing the hotel and its history. Others ask for a collection of photographs of the hotel's many features. Still others ask for recipes from the restaurants located in the Magnolia, Cascade, Conservatory, and Delta areas of the Opryland Hotel.

We listened to our guests, and the result is this book, which, I hope, addresses these various needs. In response to our guests' requests, we've created *A Taste of Tradition*. Indeed, this is a book designed with our guests in mind. It is a collection of general information, some history, a few facts and figures, and a bit of trivia about the Opryland Hotel. Coupled with the information are many colorful photographs of several of the hotel's marvelous attractions.

We didn't stop there. Included in these pages are those most frequently requested recipes from our award-winning chefs. Now our readers can sample some of the food that has won worldwide acclaim and daily delights our guests.

We hope you enjoy *A Taste of Tradition*. We believe this book will let you and your family and friends experience the Opryland Hotel's grand tradition in your homes for years to come.

Shirlee Lawrence-Verploegen
Publisher
Buyer/Manager, Retail

The Winner's Circle

Richard Gerst joined Opryland Hotel in 1978 as a Sous Chef in the Old Hickory Restaurant; he was promoted to evening senior Sous Chef of the main kitchen in 1982, to Executive Sous Chef in 1984, and to Executive Chef in 1988. His background includes positions with Princess Hotel in Hamilton, Bermuda; Sport Hotel Meierhof in Davos Dorf, Switzerland; Hotel Chaumont et Golf in Neuchatel, Switzerland; and Residence and Edenwolff hotels in Munich, West Germany.

Behind every successful performance, there is a dedicated cast of supporting players. Working outside the spotlight to silent applause, their reward is simply knowing that because of their labors, the show will go on.

My Culinary Staff is comprised of 26 Sous Chefs, 30 Apprentices, and 80 Pantry Helpers who bring each restaurant to life and each banquet to fruition. Each special occasion is given its own unique personality for lasting memories.

It is my job to orchestrate this massive piece of music. Serving 5,000 guests in a single banquet is a science—one that we have perfected and do often. Our culinary team accepts the challenge every day to continue to enrich the tradition of excellence Opryland Hotel has established since 1977. We are committed to living up to the fine reputation which we have built over the years.

I sincerely hope that you will enjoy this cookbook, which includes a tasteful sampling of the menu items frequently requested by our guests.

Richard Gerst

Richard Gerst
Executive Chef

Preface

The Opryland Hotel in Nashville, Tennessee, was born to a grand tradition in 1977, and that tradition continues today. Building a hotel into a distinctive world-class convention and vacation property that appeals to business and pleasure travelers alike isn't unlike creating a masterpiece in the kitchen. Both require just the right mix of ingredients.

An interesting history, beautiful facilities, an assortment of special services and recreational outlets, a staff dedicated to extending the finest hospitality imaginable, and first-class restaurants offering excellent food and beverages are among the ingredients necessary for creating an award-winning hotel. The Opryland Hotel is blessed with an abundance of dining facilities that have helped shape it into a hospitality industry masterpiece.

This book is a collection of recipes featured in the Opryland Hotel's world-class restaurants. *A Taste of Tradition* offers readers a chance to sample some of the fare that guests visiting the hotel enjoy daily.

A Taste of Tradition, however, is more than a cookbook. It also includes a wealth of information describing the history and unprecedented growth of the Opryland Hotel. In a sense, this book offers readers a glimpse of the "recipe" used to create the award-winning Opryland Hotel.

So sit back and enjoy this taste of the Opryland Hotel's tradition.

Hotel Awards

Chef Richard Gerst has won numerous awards in state, national, and international culinary competitions, including a gold medal in the 1981 National Restaurant Association Show.

AAA
Four Diamond Award to Chat and Chew, Employee
Cafeteria, 1988-1994

American Academy of Restaurant and Hospitality
Five Diamond Best of Best Award, 1994
Five Star Diamond Award, 1993, 1994

American Culinary Federation's
National Junior Member of the Year
Jennifer Salmon, 1996

ASAE
Prima Award, 1993, 1995

Corporate Meetings and Incentives Magazine
10 Best Hotels for Excellence, 1983-1992

Corporate and Incentive Travel Magazine
Award of Excellence, 1984-1995

Council on Hotel, Restaurant & Institutional Education
Silver Partner Award, 1994

Incentive Magazine
Platinum Award, 1993, 1994

Kraft Foods
First Place Award for Culinary Apprenticeship
Southeastern Section of the
United States, 1990, 1992, 1996

Special Events Magazine
Best Event Coordinated by a
Hotel Catering Department, 1994

Lodging Hospitality
Design Circle Awards - Best New Restaurant,
Cascades Terrace, 1989

Meeting and Conventions Magazine
Gold Key Award, 1980-1996
Gold Key Hall of Fame, 1991, 1994
Gold Platter Award, 1984, 1986, 1991, 1993-1996
Gold Tee Award, 1991-1994
Image Award, 1992

Mobile Travel Guide
Four Star Award, 1979-1986
Three Star Award, 1987-1990

Nashville Scene
Best Sunday Brunch, 1993, 1994
Best Place to Take Out-of-Towners, 1993, 1994

Restaurant Hospitality Magazine
500 Achievement, 1980-1985
Top of the Table Award, 1982, 1987-1989

Successful Meetings Magazine
Pinnacle Award, 1985-1996

Tennessee Meeting Professionals International
TMPI Facility of the Year, 1994

Tennessee Restaurant Association
Cascades Lunch, Second, 1995
Old Hickory Dinner, First, 1995

Introduction

When the Opryland Hotel opened in 1977, few people realized that a single decision made in the mid-1970s would change the course of Nashville forever, transforming it into a premier meeting and convention destination.

Developers of Opryland initially wanted to build a 300-room motor lodge for tourists visiting Opryland Themepark and the Grand Ole Opry. Another thought was of an "inn" concept. Recognizing the area's potential for hotel catering to national conventions, Opryland officials quickly realized that a convention hotel was the only way to go. After all, a major convention hotel would appeal to pleasure travelers as well. The rest, as they say, is history.

Today, the world-famous Opryland Hotel in Nashville, Tennessee, is one of the largest and most distinctive hotel and convention centers in the nation. With the completion of the Delta expansion in 1996, the Opryland Hotel became the largest combined hotel/convention center under one roof in the entire world!

As of this writing, the Opryland Hotel can boast it is the seventh-largest hotel in the country and the largest outside of Las Vegas. The hotel portion of the Opryland USA complex now covers approximately 50 acres. Guests can choose between 15 restaurants, 10 lounges, 30 retail shops and three swimming pools.

The Opryland Hotel today has 2,883 guest rooms, more than 85 meeting rooms, five ballrooms (including the 55,269-square-foot Delta Ballroom), and the 288,000-square-foot Ryman Exhibit Hall. In all, it has 600,000 square feet of meeting and exhibit space.

With more meeting, exhibit, and public space than any other hotel in the country, the Opryland Hotel can meet the requirements of 95 percent of the nation's 10,000 trade shows and exhibitions conducted annually in the United States.

The evolution of the Opryland Hotel into the world's largest combined hotel/convention center under one roof is a fascinating story.

On November 27, 1977, the 600-room Opryland Hotel, with its blend of colonial Williamsburg and southern plantation architectural styles, opened adjacent to the Opryland Themepark and Grand Ole Opry House.

With its 600 rooms, 200 more than any other Nashville hotel, along with a 20,000-square-foot ballroom, a 30,000-square-foot Ryman Exhibit Hall for trade shows, and 20 dedicated meeting rooms, the Opryland Hotel instantly became Tennessee's largest convention hotel. Because the hotel could accommodate such large convention groups, it would help make Nashville a year-round convention and meeting center.

In 1983, the hotel's $55 million Phase II expansion added 467 rooms for a total of 1,067; the Conservatory, a two-acre tropical garden under glass; and 71,000 square feet of exhibit space.

The European-inspired Conservatory is accented by a one-acre skylight that connects two six-story wings of guest rooms and houses some 10,000 tropical plants. Guests can stroll along its streams and view its waterfalls from the ground level as well as from an elevated promenade level.

Five years later, the hotel's $65 million Phase III expansion added 824 rooms for a total of 1,891, making it the 12th-largest hotel in the nation. Also added was the two-acre water-themed Cascades area. Three waterfalls ranging from 23 to 35 feet tall rumble from the top of a 40-foot-tall mountain into a 12,500-square-foot lake.

At the opposite end of the lake is the Cascades Restaurant, which has a tropical flair, and in the middle is the Cascades Terrace, a revolving lounge. The restaurant and lounge are separated by the "Dancing Waters" fountain that is accented by lasers and colored incandescent lights. Elaborate computers control the "Dancing Waters" shows, some of which are synchronized to music.

In 1993, with more than two million advance room nights already on the books and an occupancy rate averaging better than 85 percent, the Opryland Hotel at its present size was virtually at capacity.

That year, the hotel announced plans for a $175 million project, the largest construction project in Nashville history. This Phase IV expansion project doubled the hotel's trade show facilities; added 992 guest rooms, for a total of 2,883; and created a 4.5-acre glass-covered public space called the Delta.

June 1996 marked the "Dawning of the Delta" at the Opryland Hotel. With more restaurants, retail shops, and a lake and river system ranging from 14- to 25-feet wide and two feet deep, the Delta is a magnificent addition.

At 4.5 acres, the Delta is bigger than the hotel's two existing gardens, the Conservatory, and the Cascades, combined. Like them, though, the Delta was designed specifically so that guests can relax between meetings in a park-like setting, complete with waterfalls and fountains.

The Delta's glass roof overhead weighs 650 tons and soars to a peak of 150 feet. The space is so big that it accommodates a collection of two- and three-story buildings that contain shops, restaurants, lounges, and meeting rooms.

This indoor garden boasts hundreds of sabal palms, West Indian mahoganies, Southern magnolias, camellias, ever-blooming gardenias, and black olive trees complete with Spanish moss hanging from the branches of the trees. The setting is reminiscent of the sub-tropical Mississippi River Delta.

A visual highlight of the Delta is a colonaded, two-story antebellum house at the north end of the garden. This is Beauregard's, a 400-seat restaurant.

Another attention-getter is a circular fountain with 97 jets. The center jet sends a stream of water 85 feet into the Delta's 150-foot-high glass dome. The fountain is surrounded by a terrace that invites visitors to pause and enjoy the relaxing water show. Nearby is the Delta Island Food Court, a casual-style

dining area featuring a variety of items at six different food outlets.

The Delta is big enough that, yes, a river does run through it. The Delta River is more than a quarter of a mile long, and five flatboats carry passengers on trips of about 10 minutes' duration. The boats, resembling Mississippi flatboats, can carry up to 25 passengers, and one has been adapted so it can carry objects as large as an automobile for display to visitors on the Delta's walkways.

As the Opryland Hotel has grown, so has the list of services it offers its guests. In 1989 the hotel added a fitness center for guests and an upscale Magnolia Ballroom. In 1991 the hotel spent $3.1 million to add 38,431 square feet of meeting and office space east of the Magnolia Lobby.

A year later, the hotel opened an ice cream/confections shop near the entrance to the Conservatory. Modeled after Europe's famous sidewalk cafes, this new dining option would become the Conservatory Cafe.

Earlier in 1990, the Springhouse Golf Club opened. Designed by U.S. Open winner and two-time PGA champion Larry Nelson, this championship golf course is nestled between the Cumberland River and a bluff with 90-foot cliffs.

The Springhouse's 18-hole golf course covers 220 acres, and its layout and earthen mounds are a traditional links-style design. Not only do guests enjoy this world-class golf course, some of golfing's finest senior players compete annually in the

BellSouth Senior Classic at Opryland, a PGA Senior Tour event.

Complementing the golf course's magnificent greens is a clubhouse complete with a restaurant, a golf shop, locker rooms, and meeting space. Even non-golfers enjoy the special Springhouse Sunday brunch.

Other special services for hotel guests include an automated teller machine for banking needs, a business center, a rental car desk, and a full-service travel agency.

While the hotel was growing, it also was adding special events. In 1984 "A Country Christmas" was born. This highly successful annual holiday festival celebrated its 10th anniversary by spilling over into Opryland Themepark when "Christmas in the Park" began in 1993. Each year, Opryland Hotel guests are greeted by more than two million lights outside the hotel and holiday decorations throughout the interior.

Year-round, some of Nashville's finest entertainers perform in various locations throughout the hotel, and guests can even catch a glimpse of some of country music's biggest stars, who often drop by the WSM-AM Radio studio located just off the Magnolia Lobby of the hotel.

Since opening in 1977, the Opryland Hotel has captured hundreds of awards and is recognized by national trade publications as one of the nation's premier meeting and convention destinations. Foremost among these awards are honors for the hotel's food and beverage service.

A variety of dining opportunities complement the Opryland Hotel's entertainment. Whether casual or elegant, all the restaurants and the hotel's famous Sunday brunches in Rhett's and at the Springhouse Golf Club are overseen by an award-winning culinary staff.

Many of the hotel's chefs are trained in our own highly successful Opryland Culinary Institute, which was voted the best culinary apprentice program in the nation in 1995, only five years after awarding diplomas to its first seven graduates.

The hotel serves more than four million meals annually, often feeding several thousand people simultaneously. Indeed, fine dining has been and still is an essential part of the Opryland Hotel's tradition. Southern hospitality is another.

With future bookings well into the next century, the world-famous Opryland Hotel will continue to introduce millions of guests to a taste of its grand tradition of fine dining, southern hospitality, special services, and world-class facilities for many years to come.

Jack Vaughn
President
Opryland Hospitality & Attractions Group

THE MAGNOLIA

The Magnolia area of Opryland Hotel
represents the original portion of the hotel, which opened
in 1977. With its blend of Williamsburg and southern-plantation
architectural styles, the Magnolia offers the classic decor of a fine old
mansion that is both comfortable and inviting, and immediately establishes
the friendly atmosphere of the hotel. The Magnolia Lobby is the center of
activity for hundreds of thousands of conventioneers, trade show delegates,
and leisure travelers. Its main features are the grand staircase and two
massive fireplaces that extend four and one-half stories.

Visitors to the Magnolia area are able to enjoy its fine collection of Tennessee
art, assembled through two juried competitions. The collection includes
oils, photographs, pastels, charcoals and watercolors. The Magnolia
mezzanine features a continually updated portrait series of
Grand Ole Opry stars by artist John Black.

THE
MAGNOLIA

The Old Hickory Traditional Steakhouse

The Old Hickory Traditional Steakhouse is one of the hotel's most popular restaurants. Its decor recalls that of a grand dining room in Andrew Jackson's day, but the arrangement is divided into four main dining areas with private seating alcoves in order to create a warmer, more intimate atmosphere. For more casual dining, Rachel's Kitchen offers traditional family food, serving breakfast, lunch, and dinner in its large dining room and patio.

For entertainment, the Magnolia offers the Pickin' Parlor, an old-time saloon. Right off the main lobby, the studio of WSM-AM, gives guests a rare opportunity to watch Music City in action. Shopping is a main attraction in the Magnolia area featuring the Country Christmas Shoppe, men's clothing at Derringer's, Miss Scarlett's Jewelry and Gifts, the Nashville Gallery and the Clock Shop. Ramon of California is in this area and features all the finest beauty services for both men and women.

Lobster Claw Appetizers

12	ounces lobster claw meat
1	shallot, minced
	Chopped fresh tarragon leaves
1	tablespoon vegetable oil
½	cup riesling
½	cup heavy cream
4	to 6 (3-inch) round puff pastry shells
1	egg yolk
1	to 2 teaspoons butter
	Salt and pepper to taste
	Shredded Cheddar cheese
	Sprigs of fresh tarragon
4	to 6 lemon wedges

Clean the lobster claw meat, leaving it in large chunks.

Sauté the shallot and chopped tarragon in the oil in a sauté pan. Cook until the shallots are tender. Add the wine. Cook until reduced by ⅔. Add the cream. Cook until reduced by ⅔ or until of the desired consistency. Remove from the heat.

Place the pastry shells on a baking sheet. Brush with the egg yolk. Bake at 375 degrees until golden brown.

Melt the butter in a large sauté pan. Add the lobster. Sauté until heated through. Season with salt and pepper. Stir in the wine sauce a small amount at a time. Keep warm.

Place 1 hot pastry shell on each plate. Cut a hole in the top, reserving the top for use as a garnish. Spoon the lobster into the pastries. Spoon the wine sauce over the lobster and around the plate. Sprinkle with cheese. Top with the pastry shell tops. Garnish with tarragon sprigs and lemon wedges.

Four to Six Servings

The Old Hickory Traditional Steakhouse

Andrew "Old Hickory" Jackson established the tradition of fine foods attractively served in beautiful surroundings at the Hermitage, and the Old Hickory Steakhouse at Opryland Hotel carries on that tradition. The recipes on the following pages include some of the classics that you will find on the menu there. Reservations are advisable for the restaurant.

Apple Zucchini Soup

1	large zucchini, coarsely chopped
1	onion, coarsely chopped
2	Granny Smith apples, peeled, chopped
5	tablespoons butter
¾	cup flour
1½	quarts chicken stock
	Whipping cream to taste
	Salt and pepper to taste
1	apple, thinly sliced

❖ ❖ ❖

Sauté the zucchini, onion and chopped apples in 1 tablespoon of the butter in a skillet until the onion is translucent. Pour into a food processor or blender container. Process until puréed.

Make a roux by cooking the remaining 4 tablespoons butter and flour in a saucepan until golden brown, stirring constantly.

Add the chicken stock to the roux. Bring to a boil. Add the vegetable mixture. Simmer for 15 minutes. Stir in the whipping cream. Season with salt and pepper.

Ladle into soup bowls. Garnish with the apple slices.

Six to Eight Servings

Cream of Asparagus Soup

1	cup butter
1	large onion, minced
1	rib celery, minced
1	cup (about) flour
2	to 3 quarts water or chicken stock
	Chicken base or chicken bouillon to taste
	Salt and pepper to taste
2	to 4 cups heavy cream
2	cups chopped asparagus

❖ ❖ ❖

Melt the butter in a soup pot. Add the onion and celery. Sauté until tender. Add enough of the flour gradually to absorb the butter. Cook for 10 to 15 minutes or until browned, stirring constantly.

Stir in the water. Bring to a boil; reduce the heat. Season with the chicken base, salt and pepper. Add the cream and asparagus. Cook for 10 to 15 minutes or until of the desired consistency, stirring frequently.

Ten to Fifteen Servings

The Opryland Hotel is one of only 25 hotels and resorts in the United States to receive a 1995 Gold Platter Award, which recognizes excellence in all aspects of food and beverage service for convention groups. This was the third year in a row and the sixth out of ten times the awards have been made that the hotel was selected. The criteria include quality of food presentation, creativity of menu, excellence of waiter service, and professionalism of the catering staff.

The hotel's double-duty flagpole-Christmas tree is located on a lawn northwest of the Magnolia entrance. The 141-foot pole serves as the support for the 30-by-40-foot flag during most of the year. It is raised and lowered by an internal electrical gear system and takes about ten minutes to reach the top of the pole. During the holiday season, however, the flag features 23,040 colored lights that flash on and off and transform it into a giant Christmas tree.

Gazpacho

3	tomatoes, peeled, finely chopped
1	cucumber, peeled, finely chopped
1	red onion, finely chopped
1	clove of garlic, finely chopped
¼	teaspoon cumin
¼	teaspoon basil
¼	teaspoon marjoram
¼	cup red wine vinegar
¼	cup olive oil
2	cups vegetable juice cocktail
1	cup beef stock
	Tabasco sauce to taste
	Salt to taste
	Chopped fresh cilantro

❖ ❖ ❖

Combine the tomatoes, cucumber, onion, garlic, cumin, basil, marjoram, vinegar, olive oil, vegetable juice cocktail, beef stock, Tabasco sauce and salt in a large bowl and mix well. Adjust the seasonings.

Chill thoroughly.

Ladle into bowls. Garnish with cilantro.

Four Servings

Southern Velvet Soup

2	bay leaves
¼	bunch parsley, chopped
2	teaspoons black peppercorns
2	teaspoons white peppercorns
3	sprigs of fresh thyme
½	cup butter
4	cups chopped celery
2	cups chopped onions
1	quart oysters
¼	cup brandy
1	cup clam juice
2¼	cups fish stock
2	cups cream
½	cup butter
1½	cups flour
	Salt and pepper to taste
½	cup sherry

❖ ❖ ❖

Tie the bay leaves, parsley, black peppercorns, white peppercorns and thyme in a cheesecloth bag to make a bouquet garni.

Melt ½ cup butter in a stockpot. Add the bouquet garni, celery, onions and oysters. Sauté until the celery and onions are tender.

Add the brandy, stirring to deglaze the stockpot. Add the clam juice and fish stock. Cook over medium heat for 45 to 60 minutes or until the oysters are cooked through. Strain through a sieve, reserving the soup stock and removing the bouquet garni.

Return the oysters, celery, onions and soup stock to the stockpot. Stir in the cream. Cook until heated through.

Melt ½ cup butter in a saucepan or skillet. Add the flour. Cook until the flour is browned, stirring constantly. Add to the soup and mix well. Season with salt and pepper. Stir in the sherry.

Ten Servings

Alaskan Seafood Chowder

1	pound each Alaskan cod fillets, pollock fillets and salmon fillets
2	pounds Alaskan snow crab legs
3	cups chopped onions
	White portion of 2 medium leeks, sliced
4	cloves of garlic, minced
	Vegetable oil for sautéing
7	cups clam juice
3	cups chicken stock
2	cups chopped canned tomatoes
2	cups water
	Juice of 2 lemons
1	tablespoon crushed thyme
2	teaspoons red pepper flakes
2½	teaspoons crushed saffron
⅛	teaspoon white pepper, or to taste
2	bay leaves
2	cups chopped potatoes, cooked
3	cups corn kernels
¼	cup chopped parsley

❖ ❖ ❖

Remove skin and bones from the fish; cut the fish into pieces. Remove the crab meat from the shells; cut into 1-inch pieces. Cover and chill until needed.

Sauté the onions, leeks and garlic in oil in a medium stockpot over medium heat until tender. Stir in the clam juice, chicken stock, undrained tomatoes, water, lemon juice, thyme, red pepper, saffron, white pepper and bay leaves. Bring to a boil; reduce the heat. Simmer for 15 minutes.

Add the fish, potatoes and corn. Return to a boil; reduce the heat. Simmer, covered, for 5 minutes. Stir in the crab meat. Simmer, covered, for 2 to 3 minutes or until the crab meat is heated through and the fish is cooked through. Remove and discard the bay leaves. Garnish with the parsley.

Twelve to Sixteen Servings

Cucumber Crab Soup

2 pounds snow crab meat
3 cucumbers, peeled, seeded
2 tablespoons white wine
1 tablespoon chopped dill
2 cups sour cream
1 teaspoon Worcestershire sauce
2 tablespoons lobster base
   Freshly squeezed lemon juice to taste
   Salt and pepper to taste
5 to 6 green or red bell peppers

Combine the crab meat, cucumbers, wine, dill, sour cream, Worcestershire sauce, lobster base, lemon juice, salt and pepper in a food processor container. Blend until smooth. Chill until serving time.

Clean 1 bell pepper per serving. Cut off tops and fill with the soup.

Five to Six Servings

It's always Christmas in one special corner of Opryland Hotel. Tucked away in the Magnolia Galleria, the Country Christmas Shoppe is pure holiday magic. The ornaments and gifts there, many especially geared to men, make the perfect souvenir for guests and their friends and families. Items with prices from $1.95 to over $1,000 include ornaments, nativity sets, crafts, and collectibles.

Crisp Iceberg Lettuce Fantasy for Two

Fantasy Dressing
¼ cup chopped onion
2 tablespoons chopped pimento
1 tablespoon chopped chives
¼ cup boiling water
2 tablespoons sugar
    Salt and white pepper to taste
1 tablespoon Worcestershire sauce
6 tablespoons white vinegar
½ cup salad oil

Salad
½ head crisp iceberg lettuce, cut into wedges
2 ounces Monterey Jack, Cheddar or Swiss cheese, diced
8 fried onion rings
4 cherry tomatoes
2 radishes
2 carrot sticks

❖ ❖ ❖

For the dressing, combine the onion and pimento in a food processor container. Process until mixed. Stir in the chives.

Mix the boiling water, sugar, salt and pepper in a large bowl. Add the onion mixture, Worcestershire sauce and vinegar and mix well. Stir in the oil gradually.

For the salad, arrange the lettuce over a large platter. Top with the cheese, onion rings, cherry tomatoes, radishes and carrot sticks. Serve with the dressing.

Two Servings

For an Opryland Lettuce Wedge Salad, add 2 tomato slices to the crisp lettuce quarter. Overlap 3 onion rings on the tomato slices and top with black olives.

Mushroom Salad Timberland

Blueberry Vinaigrette
1   cup fresh or thawed frozen blueberries
½   cup white wine vinegar
¼   cup sugar
Salad
2   tablespoons butter
4   ounces assorted cultivated wild mushrooms, sliced
12   leaves Bibb lettuce
8   leaves red oak leaf lettuce
8   leaves Belgian endive
4   small leaves radicchio
8   pitted black olives
½   (3-ounce) package enoki mushrooms

❖ ❖ ❖

For the vinaigrette, combine the blueberries, vinegar and sugar in a blender container. Process until smooth. Strain into a cup and set aside.

For the salad, heat the butter in a large skillet over medium heat. Add the wild mushrooms. Sauté for 2 minutes or until tender. Add the dressing. Cook over low heat just until warmed, stirring constantly. Remove from the heat.

Divide the Bibb lettuce, red lettuce, Belgian endive, radicchio and olives among the plates. Add the enoki mushrooms and the warm mushrooms with dressing.

Four Servings

German Sauerbraten

Marinade

3	cups white vinegar
3	cups water
1	carrot, sliced
1	onion, chopped
3	bay leaves
10	cloves
15	peppercorns
2	tablespoons pickling spice

Beef

1	(5-pound) beef rump roast
	Salt to taste
5	tablespoons vegetable oil
2	onions, sliced
1	tablespoon tomato paste
1	bay leaf
6	cloves
3	tablespoons butter
3	tablespoons flour
½	tablespoon sugar
	Pepper to taste

❖ ❖ ❖

For the marinade, combine the vinegar, water, carrot, onion, bay leaves, cloves, peppercorns and pickling spice in a saucepan. Bring to a boil and simmer for 5 minutes. Cool to room temperature.

For the beef, season the roast with salt and place in a glass dish or bowl. Pour the marinade over the top. Add additional water and vinegar if needed to cover the beef completely. Marinate in the refrigerator for 5 days, turning twice daily.

Drain, reserving the marinade. Dry the beef well. Brown on all sides in the heated oil in a large roasting pan. Remove the beef.

Add the onions to the pan. Cook until brown. Stir in the tomato paste. Cook for several minutes longer.

During "Country Christmas" at Opryland Hotel, the Magnolia entrance is illuminated with twinkling white lights that line the driveway from the entrance driveway right up to the front door. The Magnolia Lobby is host to a 25-foot poinsettia tree around which guests gather to listen to the pianist, who plays daily during the holiday season.

Return the beef to the pan. Strain the marinade into the pan to reach halfway up the beef. Add the bay leaf and cloves. Bring to a boil and reduce the heat. Simmer, tightly covered, for 3½ to 4 hours, turning several times and adding additional marinade if needed.

Remove the beef to a warm platter. Skim the cooking liquid, discarding the bay leaf and cloves; set aside.

Melt the butter in a saucepan. Stir in the flour and sugar. Cook over low heat until caramel brown, stirring constantly. Stir in the cooking liquid. Cook for 20 minutes, stirring occasionally.

Return the beef to the saucepan. Cook for 10 minutes longer, adding marinade if needed for the desired consistency. Season with salt and pepper.

Serve with Potato Dumplings (page 136).

Ten Servings

Black Bean and Corn Salsa

¼	cup olive oil
¼	cup chopped onion
1	tablespoon minced garlic
2	cups cooked black beans
½	cup chopped tomato
1	cup cooked corn
½	tablespoon chopped jalapeño
1	tablespoon cumin
½	cup white wine
½	cup lime juice
	Salt and pepper to taste

❖ ❖ ❖

Heat the olive oil in a sauté pan. Add the onion, garlic, beans, tomato, corn and jalapeño. Stir in the cumin, wine and lime juice. Season with salt and pepper. Keep warm until serving time.

Four to Five Cups

Southwestern Filets with Black Bean and Corn Salsa and Maui Onion Rings

Red Pepper Oil
1 cup soybean oil
1 cup chopped jalapeño peppers
Onion Rings
¼ cup flour
  Garlic powder, salt, cayenne and black pepper to taste
3 onions, sliced into rings
  Vegetable oil for frying
Beef
5 (8-ounce) beef filets
  Vegetable oil
  Salt, pepper and garlic powder to taste
  Black Bean and Corn Salsa (page 35)

❖ ❖ ❖

For the pepper oil, heat the soybean oil and jalapeños in a skillet until very hot. Let cool. Process in a blender until puréed. Let the oil rise to the top. Set aside.

For the onion rings, mix the flour, garlic powder, salt, cayenne and black pepper in a bowl. Dredge the onion rings in the flour mixture. Heat oil to 350 degrees in a skillet. Add the onion rings. Fry until golden brown.

Rub the filets with vegetable oil, salt, pepper and garlic powder. Cook by the method of your choice until done to taste.

Spoon the salsa onto plates. Top with the filets. Top with generous portions of onion rings. Squirt the red pepper oil around the filets.

Five Servings

Beef Wellington

Stuffing

16	ounces white mushrooms, minced
2	tablespoons minced shallots
1	teaspoon minced fresh garlic
¼	cup butter
¼	cup sherry
	Salt and pepper to taste

Beef

4	(6-ounce) filets mignons
	Salt and pepper to taste
4	(8x8-inch) sheets puff pastry
8	ounces goose liver pâté, cut into 4 slices
1	egg, beaten
1	tablespoon cold water

❖ ❖ ❖

For the stuffing, combine the mushrooms, shallots, garlic and butter in a large sauté pan over medium heat. Cook for 15 to 20 minutes or until all the moisture has evaporated, stirring frequently. Remove from the heat.

Stir in the sherry. Cook until no liquid is visible on the bottom of the pan. Season with salt and pepper. Cool to room temperature.

For the beef, season the filets with salt and pepper. Place in a skillet. Sear over medium-high heat. Pan sauté or char-grill until browned.

Place the pastry sheets on a floured board. Place 1 pâté slice in the center of each pastry. Spread each with 2 tablespoons of the stuffing. Top with the filets.

Mix the egg and cold water in a cup. Brush some of the egg wash over the edges of the pastry. Fold the edges as for an envelope to seal. Turn upright and brush with remaining egg wash.

Bake at 350 degrees until browned.

Four Servings

The average housekeeper at Opryland Hotel makes up 32 beds a day, so he or she is bound to run into an occasional wrinkle. You might imagine, however, how one employee felt upon walking into an empty room and finding life-sized elves tucked into bed. The elves, it turned out, had been stolen from a "Country Christmas" exhibit and reported missing the day before.

Veal with Wild Rice

Wild Rice
¼   cup butter
2   tablespoons minced shallots
1   tablespoon minced garlic
1½   cups rice
¼   cup wild rice
¼   cup white wine
4   cups chicken stock
   Salt and pepper to taste

Marsala Sauce
1   cup sliced chanterelle mushrooms
1   cup sliced portobello mushrooms
1   cup sliced shiitake mushrooms
3   tablespoons minced shallots
1   tablespoon minced garlic
2   tablespoons butter
¾   cup marsala
1¼   cups veal glacé
   Salt and pepper to taste

Veal
5   (6-ounce) veal scalopini

❖ ❖ ❖

For the rice, heat the butter in a medium ovenproof saucepan. Add the shallots, garlic, rice and wild rice. Sauté for 2 minutes.

Add the wine, chicken stock, salt and pepper. Bring to a boil. Bake at 350 degrees for 25 to 30 minutes or until tender.

For the sauce, sauté the mushrooms, shallots and garlic in the butter in a saucepan for 2 minutes. Add the wine, stirring to deglaze the pan. Cook until the liquid is reduced by half. Add the veal glacé. Simmer for 5 minutes. Season to taste.

For the veal, cut each scalopini into 2-ounce portions. Pound very thin. Sauté in a nonstick skillet until golden brown.

Place the rice in the center of the serving plates. Top with the veal. Spoon the marsala sauce over the top.

Five Servings

Banquet Setup employees once went through 10 tons of trash to find a crystal peach that a client had lost. Another day, those same employees searched through 15 tons of garbage to locate a meeting planner's notebook. The department once built a special stage to show Tennessee Walking Horses in the Presidential Ballroom and another time they set up a ballroom for a pig race.

Rack of Lamb Old-Hickory Style

1	(8-bone) rack of lamb, Frenched
2	tablespoons sherry
2	tablespoons dry English mustard
	Dijon mustard to taste
2	slices bread, crusts trimmed
1	teaspoon finely chopped fresh parsley
1	teaspoon finely chopped fresh rosemary
1	teaspoon finely chopped fresh mint
1	teaspoon finely chopped fresh thyme
1	teaspoon finely chopped fresh oregano
1	teaspoon finely chopped fresh basil
6	tablespoons mango chutney

❖ ❖ ❖

Sear the lamb in a hot skillet. Cover the bones with foil and place in a roasting pan. Roast at 350 degrees until slightly undercooked.

Stir the sherry into the dry mustard in a bowl. Add some of the Dijon mustard if the mixture is too spicy. Set aside.

Process the bread to crumbs in a food processor. Add the parsley, rosemary, mint, thyme, oregano and basil. Process until mixed.

Spread the mustard mixture over the lamb. Top with the chutney; cover with the bread crumbs.

Bake until the bread crumbs are browned. Remove the foil from the bones and serve with tarragon-mint lamb glacé or lamb sauce.

Six to Eight Servings

Pork Medallions Citrus

3	oranges
3	lemons
3	limes
1	cup boiling water
1	teaspoon cornstarch
	Salt and pepper to taste
16	(2-ounce) pork medallions
2	tablespoons butter

❖　❖　❖

Grate the zest of the oranges, lemons and limes. Section the fruit and reserve the sections. Blanch the zest in the boiling water in a saucepan for 2 or 3 minutes; drain, reserving the liquid.

Cook the reserved cooking liquid in a saucepan until reduced by ½. Blend the cornstarch with a small amount of water. Stir into the sauce. Cook until thickened, stirring constantly. Season with salt and pepper.

Brown the pork medallions in the butter in a nonstick skillet for 2 minutes on each side. Remove to serving plates. Sauté the reserved fruit sections lightly in the skillet. Spoon over the pork. Top with the sauce.

Eight Servings

Chicken Kiev

2	boneless skinless chicken breast halves
½	stick butter
2	tablespoons chopped chives
2	tablespoons chopped tarragon
1	clove of garlic, minced
½	teaspoon salt
¼	teaspoon white pepper
2	tablespoons (about) flour
1	egg, beaten
½	cup dry bread crumbs
	Vegetable oil for deep-frying

❖ ❖ ❖

Rinse the chicken and pat dry. Pound ¼ inch thick.

Shape the butter into a ½x2-inch log. Roll in a mixture of the chives, tarragon, garlic, salt and pepper. Cut into halves.

Place half the butter on each chicken breast. Roll the chicken to enclose the butter completely. Secure with a wooden pick if needed.

Coat the chicken with the flour and brush with the egg. Roll in the bread crumbs.

Heat oil to 360 degrees in a deep fryer. Deep-fry the chicken until golden brown. Drain on paper towels.

Two Servings

The centerpiece of the hotel's "Country Christmas" activities is a "A Down-Home Country Christmas Musical Celebration." Other attractions include a nightly "Ceremony of the Yule Log" in the Delta, a holiday version of "Dancing Waters" synchronized to Christmas music in the Cascades, and Christmas caroling by local choirs and musical groups.

Baked Stuffed Chicken

Chicken
	Breasts and wings of 3 (2-pound) chickens
1	cup plus 2 tablespoons short grain rice
	Salt and pepper to taste
6	shallots, minced
3	eggs
6	tablespoons (about) butter

Glaze
3	ribs celery, chopped
¾	cup chopped onion
¼	to ½ cup chardonnay
	Salt and pepper to taste
	Poultry seasoning to taste
6	cups (about) chicken stock
¾	cup peeled whole almonds
1	tablespoon (about) butter
	Cantaloupe melon balls
	Honeydew melon balls
	Blue seedless grapes
	White seedless grapes

❖ ❖ ❖

For the chicken, remove the bone, leaving the upper wing bones in the breasts and reserving the bones for the glaze. Rinse the chicken and pat dry.

Bring the rice, salt, pepper and shallots to a boil in a saucepan. Cook until the rice is tender; do not rinse. Let cool. Add the eggs and mix well.

Stuff the rice mixture into the chicken legs. Roll in buttered 6x8-inch sheets of foil and place in a baking pan or on a baking sheet. Bake at 350 degrees for 20 minutes.

Season the chicken breasts with additional salt and pepper. Brown in the butter in a skillet. Place in the oven with the chicken legs. Bake for 10 to 15 minutes or until cooked through.

For the glaze, coarsely chop the reserved chicken bones. Cook in a skillet over high heat until browned. Add the celery and onion. Cook until tender. Add the wine, stirring to deglaze the skillet. Add salt, pepper, poultry seasoning and chicken stock. Simmer for1 hour.

Strain the cooking liquid. Return to the skillet and return to a boil. Skim the top carefully. Cook until reduced to ¾ cup.

Sauté the almonds in the butter until lightly browned. Add the melon balls and grapes. Sauté briefly. Add the chicken stock mixture. Bring to a boil.

Place 1 chicken breast in the center of each plate. Slice the chicken legs diagonally and arrange attractively on the plates. Top with the glaze. Serve with seasonal vegetables.

Six Servings

The Legend of the Yule Log, a book written by the hotel's director of housekeeping Pat Schappert and illustrated by employee Kathy Saine, tells the origins of this delightful medieval practice and forms the basis of the ritual performed nightly during "A Country Christmas." Completely planned and performed by costumed members of the hotel staff, it is treasured by the employees as a unique opportunity to wish a "Merry Christmas" to all who visit the hotel during the holidays. The book is sold year-round in the Country Christmas Shoppe.

Chicken Fettuccini Cardinal

8	ounces fettuccini
8	cups boiling salted water
2	chicken breasts, cut into ½-inch strips
1	tablespoon butter
8	shrimp, peeled, deveined
1	clove of garlic, minced
3	shallots, chopped
1	green bell pepper, cut into thin strips
1	yellow bell pepper, cut into thin strips
1	red bell pepper, cut into thin strips
2	tablespoons Cajun seasoning, or to taste
1	cup white wine
1	cup whipping cream
2	tablespoons butter
	Green tops of 1 bunch scallions, chopped

❖ ❖ ❖

Cook the fettuccini in the boiling salted water in a saucepan for 8 minutes. Drain in a colander and rinse with cold water.

Rinse the chicken and pat dry. Sauté in 1 tablespoon butter in a medium sauté pan for 1 minute. Add the shrimp. Sauté for 3 minutes. Remove from the pan. Stir the garlic, shallots, bell pepper strips and Cajun seasoning into the pan. Add the wine. Cook over medium-high heat until reduced by ⅔. Add the whipping cream; reduce the heat.

Return the chicken and shrimp to the pan. Cook for 3 minutes or until the chicken is cooked through and the shrimp turn pink.

Heat 2 tablespoons butter in a large sauté pan until it begins to melt. Add the fettuccini. Cook until heated through, tossing to coat well.

Arrange the fettuccini on 4 plates. Top each with 2 shrimp, 3 chicken strips and ¼ of the pepper mixture. Spoon the sauce over the top. Sprinkle with the scallions.

Four Servings

Halibut Chesapeake

12   (3-ounce) halibut fillets, thinly sliced
      Salt and pepper to taste
      Worcestershire sauce and lemon juice to taste
10   tablespoons flour
5   eggs, slightly beaten
½   cup butter
2   shallots, minced
6   ounces bay scallops
6   ounces bay shrimp
9   ounces mussels
½   cup butter
2   to 3 tablespoons brandy
1   bunch fresh dill, chopped
1¼   cups Fish Velouté
6   lemons
1   bunch fresh parsley, chopped

Season the halibut with a mixture of salt, pepper, Worcestershire sauce and lemon juice. Dip in the flour, then in the eggs. Sauté in ½ cup butter in a sauté pan until golden brown and easily flaked. Arrange on plates.

Sauté the shallots, scallops, shrimp and mussels in ½ cup butter in a sauté pan. Deglaze the pan with the brandy. Stir in half the dill. Pour over the halibut.

Heat the Fish Velouté in a saucepan. Stir in the remaining dill. Adjust the seasonings. Spoon over the seafood mixture.

Peel the lemons. Cut into wedges, removing all the seeds. Roll the wedges in the parsley. Arrange beside the fish.

Six Servings

To make Fish Velouté, brown 2 tablespoons of flour in 2 tablespoons of butter for the roux. Add 2 cups of fish stock gradually and cook until thickened, stirring constantly. Cook for 15 to 20 minutes. Season with salt, strain into a bowl, and stir in ½ cup cream.

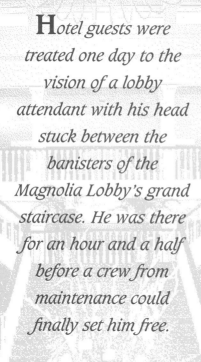

Hotel guests were treated one day to the vision of a lobby attendant with his head stuck between the banisters of the Magnolia Lobby's grand staircase. He was there for an hour and a half before a crew from maintenance could finally set him free.

Aloha Sea Bass

Mango Salsa
2   tablespoons chopped cilantro
1   teaspoon minced garlic
½   teaspoon finely chopped jalapeño pepper
¼   cup lime juice
2   large mangoes, seeded, chopped
2   tomatoes, seeded, chopped
Sweet Potato Chips
2   or 3 large sweet potatoes
     Vegetable oil for deep-frying
     Salt and pepper to taste
Strawberry Purée
1   cup strawberries
2   tablespoons sugar
1   tablespoon lime juice
Fish
5   (7-ounce) sea bass fillets
     Vegetable oil for frying

❖ ❖ ❖

For the salsa, combine the cilantro, garlic, jalapeño and lime juice in a large bowl and mix well. Add the mangoes and tomatoes. Let stand at room temperature until needed.

For the chips, slice the sweet potatoes very thin with a mandoline or vegetable slicer. Deep-fry in 325-degree oil until golden brown. Season with salt and pepper.

For the purée, combine the strawberries, sugar and lime juice in a saucepan. Cook over low heat for 5 minutes. Pour into a blender container. Process until puréed.

For the fish, brown the fillets lightly in a small amount of oil in an ovenproof sauté pan. Bake at 350 degrees for 10 minutes.

Spoon the salsa onto serving plates. Drizzle the purée around the salsa. Arrange the fish over the salsa. Top with the sweet potato chips. Garnish with additional salsa.

Five Servings

Shrimp Scampi

Garlic Sauce
1	teaspoon butter
1	tablespoon minced shallots
1	tablespoon minced fresh garlic
¾	cup chablis
2	bay leaves
½	teaspoon crushed white peppercorns
½	cup Fish Velouté (page 45) or cream of mushroom soup
1½	cups fresh cream
	Salt and pepper to taste

Shrimp
2	tablespoons butter
20	large shrimp, peeled, deveined
1	tablespoon minced fresh garlic
¼	cup chablis

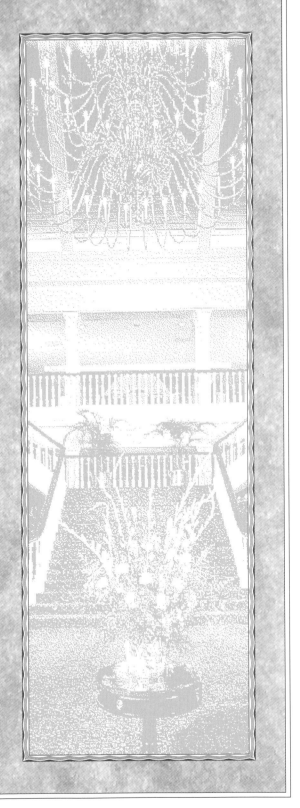

❖ ❖ ❖

For the sauce, melt the butter in a saucepan. Add the shallots and garlic. Sauté until translucent. Deglaze the pan with the chablis. Add the bay leaves and peppercorns. Cook until reduced by ½. Add the Fish Velouté and cream. Cook until the mixture coats the back of a spoon, stirring frequently. Season with salt and pepper. Strain through a sieve. Set aside and keep warm.

For the shrimp, heat the butter in a sauté pan. Stir in the shrimp. Add the garlic. Sauté until the shrimp is half cooked. Add the chablis. Cook until the shrimp turn pink; drain and discard the cooking liquid. Add the garlic sauce, stirring to coat the shrimp. Bring to a quick boil.

Serve over noodles or rice.

Four Servings

Swiss Potato Tart

1½	pounds potatoes
	Salt to taste
3	tablespoons chopped fresh basil
1½	tablespoons chopped fresh thyme
1½	tablespoons chopped fresh tarragon
3	tablespoons chopped fresh parsley
3	shallots, chopped
⅓	cup balsamic vinegar
1	cup olive oil
1	cup whipping cream
1	egg yolk, beaten
	Pepper to taste
10	ounces Swiss cheese, shredded

❖ ❖ ❖

Combine the potatoes with cold salted water to cover in a saucepan. Cook until tender and drain well. Peel the potatoes; cut into ½-inch slices.

Mix the basil, thyme, tarragon, parsley and shallots in a small bowl. Combine the vinegar and half the herb mixture in a large bowl. Whisk in the olive oil gradually. Set aside.

Beat the whipping cream in a medium bowl until soft peaks form. Fold in the egg yolk. Set aside.

Season the potatoes with salt and pepper. Toss with the remaining herb mixture and ¾ cup of the vinaigrette. Spoon onto 6 metal pastry rings set on a microwave-safe and ovenproof baking sheet. Top with the cheese, pressing down lightly. Chill for 30 minutes.

Remove the rings from the potatoes. Microwave at 50 percent power for 1 minute. Top each potato with 1 tablespoon of the whipped cream. Broil until lightly browned.

Arrange the potatoes on serving plates. Serve with a green garden salad and drizzle with the remaining vinaigrette.

Six Servings

Baked Apples

6   Granny Smith apples
        Lemon juice
½   cup packed light brown sugar
¾   teaspoon cinnamon
⅛   teaspoon nutmeg
2½   tablespoons butter, softened
1½   cups chopped dried cranberries

❖   ❖   ❖

Core the apples to but not through the bottom. Peel each apple ⅓ of the way down. Dip the apples in lemon juice.

Mix the brown sugar, cinnamon and nutmeg in a bowl. Cut in the butter until crumbly. Fill the apples with alternate layers of the brown sugar mixture and cranberries.

Place in a baking pan with a small amount of water; do not pour the water over the apples. Bake at 400 degrees for 40 minutes.

Six Servings

Preparations begin in July for the multifaceted festival known as "A Country Christmas" that opens each year at the hotel in November. Although visitors are oftened convinced that elves decorate the hotel overnight, the truth is that it takes almost 5 months to string the 2 million lights that decorate the trees and buildings for the holiday extravaganza.

Crème Brûlée

6   egg yolks
6   tablespoons sugar
⅛   teaspoon salt, or to taste
2¼   cups heavy cream
1   (1-inch) piece of vanilla bean
½   cup sugar

❖   ❖   ❖

Combine the egg yolks, 6 tablespoons sugar and salt in a heavy enameled metal or stainless steel saucepan. Set aside.

Combine the cream and vanilla bean in another saucepan. Bring to a boil, stirring occasionally to prevent scorching. Drizzle into the egg yolk mixture, stirring vigorously with a whisk or wooden spatula until mixed. Remove and discard the vanilla bean.

Cook over medium heat for 3 minutes, stirring constantly. Strain into a 4-cup enameled metal heatproof glass or porcelain baking dish. Place the baking dish in a larger baking pan. Add enough water to the pan to reach halfway up the sides of the baking dish.

Bake at 325 degrees for 35 minutes or just until the custard is set; do not overcook or allow the water in the baking pan to boil. Cool thoroughly or chill to desired temperature.

Sift ½ cup sugar ¼ inch thick over the custard. Broil until the sugar caramelizes; the top should be hard and shiny and should sound hollow when tapped.

Chill for several hours. Crack the crust when serving and serve a small amount of the crust with each portion of the custard. Serve with whipped cream if desired.

Four to Six Servings

Chocolate Marquis

1	cup butter, softened
2⅓	to 2½ cups confectioners' sugar
1	cup baking cocoa
5	egg yolks
3	ounces bittersweet chocolate, melted
1	tablespoon Grand Marnier
7	cups whipping cream
8	ounces bittersweet chocolate

❖ ❖ ❖

Cream the butter and confectioners' sugar in a large mixer bowl until light and fluffy. Add the cocoa and egg yolks and mix well. Stir in the melted chocolate and Grand Marnier.

Beat 3 cups of the whipping cream in a medium mixer bowl until soft peaks form. Fold into the chocolate mixture. Pipe into molds. Freeze until firm. Unmold onto dessert plates.

Combine the remaining 4 cups whipping cream and 8 ounces chocolate in a saucepan. Cook over medium heat until the chocolate is melted, stirring frequently. Pour over the dessert.

Four to Six Servings

The shopping list for the hotel's Christmas decorations includes 10.5 miles of evergreen garland, 7.5 miles of ribbon, 2.4 million lights, 35,000 poinsettias, nearly 100 interior Christmas trees, 26,700 tree ornaments, 175 fiberglass snowflakes in 4- to 8-foot sizes, 23 animated characters, and 155 wreaths. It takes a crew of 55 workers, electricians to string the lights, and a company of landscapers to tend the poinsettias.

Soufflé Glacé Grand Marnier

1	cup sugar
3½	tablespoons water
6	egg yolks, beaten
2½	cups whipping cream
¼	cup Grand Marnier
	Confectioners' sugar

❖ ❖ ❖

Secure a sleeve of greased paper around the outside of a soufflé mold.

Combine the sugar and water in a small saucepan. Cook until the mixture registers 245 degrees on a candy thermometer, hard-ball stage.

Add to the egg yolks gradually, whipping until the mixture is completely cooled.

Beat the whipping cream and Grand Marnier in a mixer bowl until soft peaks form. Fold into the egg yolk mixture. Pour into the prepared mold. Smooth to the edge of the paper with a spatula. Freeze for 3 hours or longer.

Sprinkle with confectioners' sugar and remove the paper sleeve.

Six to Eight Servings

Cream Cheese and Roasted Pepper Dip

1	green bell pepper
¼	cup cream cheese, softened
½	cup sour cream
¼	cup chopped onion
1	clove of garlic, chopped
	Tabasco sauce to taste
¼	teaspoon Worcestershire sauce
	Salt to taste
1	tablespoon finely chopped chives

❖ ❖ ❖

Place the green pepper in a broiler pan. Roast under the broiler until the skin is charred, turning frequently. Place in a small bowl and cover tightly with plastic wrap. Let stand until cool. Remove the skin. Peel and cut into halves, discarding the stem, inner membranes and seeds. Cut the pepper into small pieces.

Combine the cream cheese, sour cream, onion, garlic, Tabasco sauce, Worcestershire sauce and salt in a food processor container. Process until mixed.

Combine with the green pepper and chives in a bowl. Chill, covered, until serving time. Serve with bite-size fresh vegetables.

Ten to Twelve Servings

You can start your day or close out your evening at Rachel's Kitchen, a family-oriented restaurant open for breakfast, lunch, dinner, and snacks, from 6:30 in the morning to 11:00 at night during the week and until midnight on weekends. The recipes on the following pages are typical of the casual comfort food you will find at Rachel's Kitchen.

Beer Cheese Soup

1	cup butter
½	cup ground mixed sweet onions and celery
1	cup flour
8	cups chicken stock or pork stock
12	ounces Velveeta cheese, chopped, or Cheez Whiz
1	(12-ounce) bottle beer
	Salt, black pepper and red pepper flakes to taste

❖ ❖ ❖

Combine the butter, onion mixture and flour in a stockpot. Cook over low heat for 15 minutes, stirring constantly. Add the chicken stock and mix well. Cook until thickened, stirring constantly.

Add the cheese. Cook until the cheese is melted, stirring constantly. Stir in beer. Season with salt, black pepper and red pepper flakes.

Ladle into bowls. Garnish with fresh bacon bits or diced ham.

Eight to Ten Servings

Black Bean and Ham Soup

1	onion, diced
2	ribs celery, chopped
2	tablespoons butter
10	cups pork stock
2	cups dried black beans, rinsed, sorted
1	cup chopped ham
	Salt and pepper to taste
	Tabasco sauce to taste

❖ ❖ ❖

Sauté the onion and celery in the butter in a stockpot. Add the pork stock and beans. Simmer over low heat until the beans are very tender. Stir in the ham. Season with salt, pepper and Tabasco sauce.

You may thicken the soup with a mixture of melted butter and flour if desired.

Ten to Twelve Servings

One conscientious hotel housekeeper was readying a room for President Ronald Reagan and stopped by for a last-minute inspection after the Secret Service bomb-sniffing dogs left. She was horrified to find that the dogs had left a deposit on the floor! She had dropped to her knees to remove the offending deposit, when laughter informed her that the plastic deposit was the Secret Service version of humor.

Corned Beef and Cabbage Soup

1   cup (¼-inch) corned beef cubes
1   large onion, chopped
6   scallions, chopped
½   small head white cabbage, chopped
4   large potatoes, peeled, diced
8   cups chicken broth
1   cup light cream
    Salt and pepper to taste

❖ ❖ ❖

Sauté the corned beef, onion, scallions and cabbage in a large stockpot over medium heat for 5 minutes.

Add the potatoes and chicken broth. Bring to a boil; reduce the heat. Simmer, covered, for 40 minutes. Stir in the cream. Season with salt and pepper.

Ladle into bowls. Garnish with croutons sautéed in butter.

Eight to Ten Servings

You have to love the story of the house attendant-in-training who was left alone to clean the elevator cabs. After several hours, he reported to housekeeping that the elevators on the fifth and sixth floors were a lot cleaner than the ones he had cleaned on the first, second, and third floors.

Carrot and Raisin Salad

2	cups shredded carrots
½	cup raisins
½	cup chopped pecans
¼	cup honey
1	teaspoon lemon juice
½	cup miniature marshmallows
¼	cup pineapple juice

❖ ❖ ❖

Combine the carrots, raisins, pecans, honey, lemon juice and marshmallows in a large bowl and mix gently. Stir in the pineapple juice. Chill for 1 hour or longer.

Three to Four Servings

Chicken Salad

2½	cups chopped cooked chicken
½	stalk celery, chopped
½	onion, diced
2	hard-cooked eggs, chopped or sliced
1½	teaspoons Worcestershire sauce
2	tablespoons lemon juice
¼	cup white vinegar
½	cup mayonnaise
	Salt and pepper to taste

❖ ❖ ❖

Combine the chicken, celery, onion, eggs, Worcestershire sauce, lemon juice, vinegar, mayonnaise, salt and pepper in a large bowl and mix gently; do not mix until all ingredients are in the bowl.

Eight to Ten Servings

Housekeepers at Opryland Hotel find that men keep up with their belongings better than women. Of the thousands of items left behind each year, most are returned to women. Hotel officials still wonder about the artificial leg found in one room. It seems that there has never been a request for that item.

Iceberg Lettuce Chef's Salad

1	head iceberg lettuce
3	ounces smoked cheese, julienned
3	ounces turkey, julienned
3	ounces ham, julienned
¼	cup julienned mixed red and green bell pepper
3	black olives, sliced
½	hard-cooked egg, cut into wedges
4	purple onion rings

❖ ❖ ❖

Wash the lettuce and drain well. Remove the core and most of the inside leaves, leaving enough outer leaves to maintain the shape. Make a small slice on the side of the head; remove the slice so that the head can be set at an angle for viewing.

Julienne the remaining lettuce and return to the inside of the head. Top with the cheese, turkey, ham, red and green peppers, olives, egg and onion rings.

Serve with your choice of dressing.

One Serving

Honey Mustard Dressing

Peel of ½ orange, cut into thin strips
1   cup mayonnaise
2   tablespoons honey
1   tablespoon Dijon mustard
1   tablespoon Pommery mustard
Cayenne to taste

❖ ❖ ❖

Blanch the orange peel in boiling water; drain on paper towels.

Combine the mayonnaise, honey, Dijon mustard, Pommery mustard, cayenne and orange peel in a tightly covered jar and shake well.

Rachel's Kitchen serves this dressing on Fried Chicken Salad.

One Cup

Honey Mint Dressing

2   cups sour cream
1   cup crème de menthe
1½   cups honey

❖ ❖ ❖

Combine the sour cream, crème de menthe and honey in a bowl and mix until smooth and creamy.

You will find this on the Tropical Fruit Salad at Rachel's Kitchen.

Four Cups

Chili Mac

2   pounds finely chopped stew meat or ground chuck
1   cup chopped onion
1   cup chopped green pepper
1   tablespoon minced garlic
1   (16-ounce) can tomato purée
1   (8-ounce) can chopped tomatoes
¼   cup chili powder, or to taste
     Cayenne to taste
¼   teaspoon oregano
1   teaspoon cumin
1   (16-ounce) can kidney beans
     Salt and white pepper to taste
3   quarts water
2   cups macaroni, cooked

❖ ❖ ❖

Brown the stew meat in a stockpot; drain well. Add the onion and green pepper. Sauté until the vegetables are tender.

Add the garlic, tomato purée, tomatoes, chili powder, cayenne, oregano and cumin and mix well. Simmer for 30 minutes. Add the beans, salt, pepper and water. Simmer for 1 hour or until of the desired consistency. Stir in the macaroni.

Ten to Twelve Servings

Country Ham and Scroodles

1½	ounces uncooked scroodles
	Salt to taste
1	tablespoon minced shallots
1	ounce country ham
2	teaspoons chopped red bell pepper
1	tablespoon butter
1	cup heavy cream
1	ounce Ghetsemani cheese
2	teaspoons minced scallions

❖ ❖ ❖

Cook the scroodles in boiling salted water in a saucepan until tender; drain well.

Sauté the shallots, ham and red pepper in the butter in a skillet over medium heat, stirring in the cream gradually while cooking. Add the cheese. Add the scroodles and mix gently.

Spoon into a warm serving dish. Top with the scallions.

Four Servings

People who come to Nashville to hear music don't even have to leave the hotel. The hotel's lounges are some of the best places in town to catch some of country music's rising stars. The Jazz Bar in the Delta presents the best of jazz; the Pickin' Parlor presents acoustically-oriented music that's pure country; the Jack Daniel's Saloon offers a mix of music from Cajun to oldies but goodies.

Baked Chicken Casserole

24	mushrooms, sliced
1	medium onion, chopped
2	teaspoons minced garlic
¼	cup melted butter
2	cups white wine
2	pounds chopped cooked chicken
6	cups chicken velouté
1	cup whipping cream
	Salt and white pepper to taste
½	teaspoon ground nutmeg
1	teaspoon dried basil
1	teaspoon dried thyme
	Toasted fine brown bread crumbs
2	teaspoons paprika
¼	cup melted butter

❖ ❖ ❖

Sauté the mushrooms, onion and garlic in ¼ cup butter in a large saucepan over high heat for 1 minute, tossing constantly; reduce the heat to medium.

Add the white wine and chicken. Simmer for 5 minutes or until most of the liquid has evaporated. Stir in the chicken velouté; increase the heat. Bring to a boil; reduce the heat to medium. Add the cream, salt, pepper, nutmeg, basil and thyme.

Spoon into a glass baking dish. Top with a mixture of the bread crumbs and paprika. Drizzle with ¼ cup butter. Bake at 350 degrees for 15 minutes.

You may prepare chicken velouté using the recipe for Fish Velouté on page 45, substituting chicken stock for the fish stock.

Six Servings

Chicken and Dumplings

2   cups self-rising flour
¾   cup (about) all-purpose flour
3   to 3¼ tablespoons shortening
½   to ¾ cup milk
3   to 3¼ cups chicken broth
¾   to 1 cup chopped onion
¾   to 1 cup chopped celery
1   pound chopped cooked chicken
1   sheet puff pastry dough

❖ ❖ ❖

Combine the self-rising flour, all-purpose flour, shortening and milk in a bowl, mixing to form a soft dough. Roll on a floured surface. Cut into square dumplings.

Heat the chicken broth, onion and celery in a large pot. Drop the dumplings into the simmering mixture. Cook for 10 minutes. Add the chicken.

Spoon into an ovenproof soup tureen. Top with the puff pastry dough. Bake at 350 degrees until the puff pastry is browned.

Six Servings

To see Tennessee's river pearls, the state gem, and to learn more about the local pearl industry, which also provides most of the nuclei for Japan's pearl productions, visit Miss Scarlett's, adjacent to the Magnolia Lobby. The shop features pearls from $60 to $5,000 in unique designs, as well as a complete line of other gemstones and exclusive collectibles and gifts.

Salmon Croquettes

2	cups flaked cooked or canned salmon
2	cups mashed potatoes
1½	teaspoons salt
⅛	teaspoon pepper
1	egg, beaten
1	tablespoon minced parsley
1	teaspoon Worcestershire sauce
	Vegetable oil for deep-frying

Combine the salmon, potatoes, salt, pepper, egg, parsley and Worcestershire sauce in a bowl and mix well. Chill thoroughly.

Shape into croquettes. Deep-fry in the oil until golden brown. Drain on paper towels.

Four Servings

Big-name entertainment is provided almost daily for the hotel's convention market by the Director of Entertainment. Customized shows, with price tags ranging from $200 to $500,000, highlight such stars as Dolly Parton, Reba McEntire, and Lee Greenwood. Most of the events are, of course, staged right in the hotel, but occasional events are produced offsite, such as the Orange Bowl halftime special or international shows to promote tourism for the U.S. State Department.

Shrimp Pasta

8	ounces small shrimp, peeled, deveined
2	tablespoons chopped shallots
1	tablespoon chopped garlic
2	tablespoons clarified butter
½	cup chopped seedless cucumber
½	cup dry white wine
½	cup sour cream
½	cup heavy cream
1	pound cooked linguini
2	tablespoons chopped fresh dill
1	tablespoon chopped fresh parsley
	Salt and pepper to taste

❖ ❖ ❖

Sauté the shrimp, shallots and garlic in the butter in a large saucepan; do not brown. Add the cucumber. Add the wine, stirring to deglaze. Cook until the shrimp is almost cooked through.

Add the sour cream and cream. Bring to a boil. Add the linguini, dill, parsley, salt and pepper. Cook until the sauce is of the desired consistency. Garnish the servings with fresh dill sprigs.

Three to Four Servings

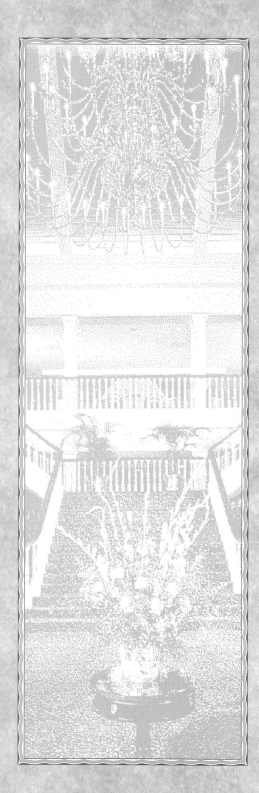

Corn Pudding

3	tablespoons butter, softened
2	tablespoons sugar
2	tablespoons flour
1	teaspoon salt
3	eggs
2	cups fresh or frozen corn
1¾	cups milk

❖ ❖ ❖

Blend the butter, sugar, flour and salt in a bowl. Add the eggs and beat well. Stir in the corn and milk.

Spoon into a buttered baking dish. Bake at 325 degrees for 45 minutes or until the top is golden brown and a knife inserted near the center comes out clean.

This may be prepared ahead and stored in a tightly covered jar in the refrigerator until baking time. Shake well before baking.

Six to Eight Servings

Fried Green Tomatoes

1	cup bread crumbs
½	tablespoon chopped thyme
½	tablespoon chopped parsley
½	tablespoon chopped oregano
2	cloves of garlic, finely chopped
2	eggs
1	cup buttermilk
	Salt and pepper to taste
3	green tomatoes, cut into ½-inch slices
1	cup flour
½	cup butter

❖ ❖ ❖

Mix the bread crumbs, thyme, parsley, oregano and garlic in a small bowl and set aside.

Combine the eggs, buttermilk, salt and pepper in a large bowl and mix well. Add the tomato slices. Let stand for 15 minutes.

Dip the tomatoes into the flour, then into the egg mixture again. Coat with the bread crumbs.

Brown on both sides in the melted butter in a cast-iron skillet. Drain on paper towels. Serve with breakfast eggs.

Three to Four Servings

Rachel's Kitchen serves Sawmill Gravy over freshly baked biscuits. To make it at home, crumble 2 sausage patties into a skillet and cook until brown. Stir in ¼ cup flour and cook for 1 minute. Stir in the milk. Simmer for 5 minutes or until thickened, stirring constantly, and season to taste.

Biscuits

4½	cups cake flour
1	tablespoon salt
3	tablespoons baking powder
¾	cup butter
1¼	cups milk

Sift the flour, salt and baking powder into a large bowl. Rub in the butter until crumbly. Add the milk, mixing to form a smooth dough.

Roll on a lightly floured surface. Cut with a biscuit cutter. Place on a baking sheet.

Bake at 400 degrees for 10 to 15 minutes or until browned.

One Dozen

Corn Sticks

½	cup flour, sifted
1½	cups self-rising cornmeal
2	teaspoons salt
2	teaspoons white pepper
3	eggs
1½	cups buttermilk
2	tablespoons bacon drippings

Mix the flour, cornmeal, salt and pepper in a medium bowl.

Beat the eggs lightly in a large bowl. Stir in the buttermilk. Add the flour mixture and blend well. Stir in the bacon drippings.

Pour into a hot greased corn stick pan. Bake at 375 degrees until golden brown.

Eight Servings

Fruit Cobbler

1	cup butter
2	cups flour
2	cups sugar
2	teaspoons baking powder
2	cups milk
4	cups mixed blackberries and raspberries, heated
1	to 2 tablespoons sugar

❖ ❖ ❖

Melt the butter in a baking pan. Mix the flour, 2 cups sugar, baking powder and milk in a bowl. Pour into the baking pan. Spoon the undrained hot fruit over the batter; do not stir.

Bake at 350 degrees for 35 minutes. Sprinkle 1 to 2 tablespoons sugar over the cobbler. Bake for 10 minutes longer.

Six to Eight Servings

Unlike most hotels, Opryland Hotel does not have a slack time, or low-occupancy time, for renovations. Their plan calls for a process of continual renovation of the guest rooms, with three shifts working around the clock to renew six rooms every twenty-four hours. The rooms are completely renewed—repainted, repapered, refurnished, recarpeted, and rebuilt from floor to ceiling, and when the last one is finished, it is time to begin again.

Pumpkin Cheesecake

10	ounces cream cheese, softened
¾	cup sugar
2	eggs
8½	ounces sour cream
4	ounces pumpkin purée
½	teaspoon cinnamon
2	tablespoons lemon juice
1	recipe cheesecake crust made with crushed graham crackers and melted butter

❖ ❖ ❖

Beat the cream cheese and sugar in a mixer bowl until smooth. Beat in the eggs 1 at a time. Add the sour cream, pumpkin and cinnamon and mix well. Stir in the lemon juice.

Spoon into the crust in a springform pan. Bake at 300 degrees for 1 hour and 20 minutes. Cool on a wire rack. Chill for several hours.

Place on a serving plate and remove the side of the springform pan.

Twelve Servings

Hotel Guest Services actually reads and acts on those comment cards that are solicited from guests. The comments are compiled and analyzed and a bulletin board posts the top ten compliments and the top ten complaints of the week. Guest comments are credited with actually changing the way the hotel operates, with examples including menu changes, the hotel's smoking policies, and the charges for the use of the shuttle.

Lemon Chess Pie

6	egg yolks
1	cup sugar
1	cup heavy cream
2	teaspoons cornmeal or almond flour
¼	cup lemon juice
½	cup melted butter
1½	tablespoons flour
1	unbaked (10-inch) pie shell

❖ ❖ ❖

Combine the egg yolks and sugar in a mixer bowl and beat until thickened and pale yellow. Add the cream, cornmeal and lemon juice and mix well. Mix in the butter and flour.

Spoon into the pie shell. Bake at 300 degrees for 30 minutes or until the center is set. Cool on a wire rack. Chill until serving time.

Eight Servings

Peanut Butter Pie

1	envelope unflavored gelatin
1	cup cold milk
¼	cup sugar
4	egg yolks
	Salt to taste
1	teaspoon vanilla extract
½	cup peanut butter
4	egg whites
½	cup sugar
½	cup whipping cream, whipped
1	baked (9-inch) pie shell
4	ounces semisweet chocolate, chopped
½	cup heavy cream

Soften the gelatin in the cold milk in a double boiler. Heat over simmering water until the gelatin dissolves. Add ¼ cup sugar, egg yolks and salt and mix just until blended. Cook until the mixture thickens enough to coat a metal spoon, stirring constantly. Remove from the heat. Beat in the vanilla and peanut butter. Chill until thickened but not firm.

Beat the egg whites until foamy. Add ½ cup sugar gradually, beating until stiff but not dry. Fold into the peanut butter mixture. Fold in the whipped cream. Spoon lightly into the pie shell. Chill until firm.

Melt the chocolate in the cream in a double boiler over simmering water, whisking to blend well. Cook until thickened and creamy, whisking constantly. Cool slightly, stirring occasionally. Spread over the pie and sprinkle with chopped peanuts. Let stand until the topping is set before serving.

Eight Servings

THE CONSERVATORY

The Conservatory is
Opryland Hotel's two-acre tropical paradise,
inspired by nineteenth-century European gardens.
It is an enclosed botanical park containing 10,000 plants
beneath a one-acre skylight. The skylight connects two six-story
wings of guest rooms with verandas that enable guests to enjoy the
view from their rooms. Visitors can stroll along the streams and view the
waterfalls from the ground level as well as from an elevated promenade
level. The award-winning garden contains one of the largest collections
of tropical plants in the country, with 457 different kinds of plants,
including 57 varieties of palms and 15 varieties of banana trees.

Although members of the horticultural staff have to rappel from cliffs to
tend some of the plants, including the bougainvillaea that covers the 72
foot Crystal Gazebo, most of the gardening is done very unobtrusively.
Much of the credit goes to sophisticated automated systems such
as the drip and sub-irrigation system with electronic timers and
digital programming that fertilizes the garden and
waters it automatically with 50,000 gallons
of well water weekly.

THE CONSERVATORY

The Conservatory Courtyard is the setting for the celebrated Sunday Brunch—an opulent buffet offering 40 to 50 selections and accented with dramatic ice sculptures by Opryland Hotel's award-winning chefs. The signature restaurant for this area is under renovation to feature fine Italian cuisine. Adjacent to the restaurant is the famous Jack Daniel's Old Time Saloon.

Major Muffin invites guests into The Conservatory Cafe, a European-style ice cream, confection, and coffee shop for visitors on the go. Other attractions at the entrance to the Conservatory area include Aunt Pitty Pat's shop for dolls, Petals Florist, the Springhouse Golf Shop, and Nature Walk, featuring gifts related to animals and nature.

MAJOR MUFFIN

Hot Brown Butler

¼	cup margarine
½	cup flour
2	cups milk, scalded
	MSG, salt and white pepper to taste
½	cup grated Parmesan cheese
2	eggs
4	slices bread, crusts trimmed, toasted
10	ounces sliced turkey breast
2	tomatoes, sliced
	Paprika to taste
8	slices bacon, crisp-fried

❖ ❖ ❖

Melt the margarine in a saucepan over very low heat. Stir in the flour. Whisk in the milk, MSG, salt, white pepper and 3 tablespoons of the cheese. Remove from the heat. Beat in the eggs.

Place the toast in a baking pan. Arrange the turkey over the toast. Spoon the sauce over the top. Sprinkle with the remaining cheese. Place the tomato slices on top and sprinkle with paprika.

Broil or bake at 425 degrees until golden brown. Arrange the bacon on top and serve immediately.

You may substitute ham for the bacon, layering it under the turkey.

Four Servings

The following pages contain recipes for some of the favorite dishes that guests have enjoyed for years at Rhett's, as well as recipes for some of the dishes that can be found on the lavish brunch buffet served in the Conservatory courtyard every Sunday. Rhett's has been replaced by an Italian restaurant, Ristorante Volare. It and Caffé Avanti, another new Italian restaurant in the courtyard, are continuing the hotel's tradition of fine dining.

Pan-Fried Black-Eyed Pea Cakes

Jalapeño Sour Cream
3 jalapeños
3 ounces sour cream

Pea Cakes
½ cup dried black-eyed peas
1½ cups cold chicken stock
1 cup flour
1 egg
¾ cup milk
½ teaspoon baking powder
¼ teaspoon baking soda
¼ cup finely chopped onion
2 tablespoons lime juice
   Tabasco sauce to taste
   Salt and pepper to taste
   Chowchow (page 79)

❖ ❖ ❖

For the jalapeño sour cream, clean and chop the jalapeños, discarding the seeds. Mix with the sour cream in a bowl; set aside.

For the pea cakes, rinse and sort the black-eyed peas. Combine with water to cover in a bowl. Let stand for 8 hours.

Drain the peas. Combine with the chicken stock in a saucepan. Cook until tender. Process ⅔ of the peas in a food processor until smooth. Combine the processed peas with the flour, egg, milk, baking powder and baking soda in a bowl and mix until smooth. Fold in the onion and remaining peas. Season with the lime juice, Tabasco sauce, salt and pepper.

Spoon quarter-sized portions into a nonstick sauté pan or griddle. Cook until brown on both sides.

Serve the pea cakes immediately with the jalapeño sour cream and chowchow.

Six Servings

Chowchow

2	cups finely chopped cabbage
½	cup finely chopped red bell pepper
½	cup finely chopped green bell pepper
½	cup chopped carrot
2	teaspoons kosher salt
1½	tablespoons brown sugar
½	cup white vinegar
1	tablespoon mustard seeds

❖ ❖ ❖

Combine the cabbage, bell peppers, carrot and salt in a bowl and mix well. Chill for 8 hours or longer. Drain well in a colander.

Combine the brown sugar, vinegar and mustard seeds in a saucepan. Bring to a boil.

Pour over the drained vegetables in a bowl and mix well. Chill for 8 hours or longer.

Six Servings

A typical shopping list for the Sunday brunch held in the Conservatory courtyard might consist of 6,500 shrimp, 250 pounds of salmon, 250 pounds of chicken, six 50-pound prime barons of beef, 25 gallons of cocktail sauce, 50 cases of oranges and grapefruit, 120 flats of strawberries, 25 cases of cantaloupes, 25 cases of honeydew melons, 100 cases of pineapple, and 50 gallons of ice cream. Preparations for the brunch begin on Friday.

White Navy Bean Soup

14	ounces dried navy beans
8	ounces ham bones
4	ounces salt pork, chopped
1	cup chopped onions
1	cup chopped leeks
1	cup chopped celery
1	clove of garlic, crushed
¼	cup bacon grease
14	cups bouillon
3	medium potatoes, chopped
1	(14-ounce) can tomatoes
	Salt and pepper to taste

❖ ❖ ❖

Rinse and sort the beans. Combine with water to cover in a bowl. Let stand for 8 hours.

Drain the beans. Combine with the ham bones and salt pork in a large saucepan. Simmer until the beans are partially cooked.

Cook the onions, leeks, celery and garlic in the bacon grease in a skillet over very low heat until tender. Add to the beans with the bouillon.

Bring the soup to a boil. Add the potatoes. Cook for 1 hour or until the beans are tender. Add the tomatoes, salt and pepper. Cook until heated through.

Garnish with parsley and croutons.

Sixteen Servings

One of the most spectacular of the plants in the Conservatory is the bougainvillea, found on the Crystal Gazebo and the Promenade. The vine, native to Central America, is grown for its cascading masses of brilliant red flowers that bloom almost continually throughout the year, fading in mid-bloom to a more subdued hue. It was named after explorer and scientist Louis Antoine de Bougainville, (1729–1811).

Plantation Corn Chowder

1	cup chopped bacon
½	cup butter
½	cup chopped onion
½	cup chopped celery
½	cup flour
1½	cups chopped potatoes
3	cups fresh or frozen corn
5	cups chicken stock
1½	cups milk
1	cup cream
	Salt and pepper to taste

❖ ❖ ❖

Sauté the bacon in a saucepan until brown. Add the butter and heat until melted. Add the onion and celery. Sauté until the vegetables are translucent. Stir in the flour. Cook for several minutes.

Add the potatoes, corn, chicken stock and milk. Bring to a boil and reduce the heat. Simmer until the potatoes are tender, stirring frequently.

Stir in the cream. Simmer for 10 to 15 minutes. Season with salt and pepper.

Eight Servings

Cream of Sweet Potato Soup

2	tablespoons minced onion
2	tablespoons butter
1	tablespoon flour
2	cups chicken or beef broth
2	cups hot milk
2	cups cooked sweet potatoes
	Salt and pepper to taste
¼	cup orange juice (optional)
	Honey to taste (optional)
¼	teaspoon each ginger, cinnamon and mace

❖ ❖ ❖

Sauté the onion in the butter in a saucepan over medium heat for 5 minutes or until translucent. Stir in the flour and reduce the heat.

Stir in the broth. Cook for 1 to 2 minutes or until bubbly, stirring constantly. Add the milk.

Combine 2 cups of the cream sauce with the sweet potatoes in a bowl and mix well. Process 2 cups at a time in a food processor or press through a sieve.

Combine the puréed mixture with the salt, pepper, orange juice and honey in a saucepan. Add a mixture of the spices. Cook just until heated through; do not boil.

You may also make this with yams, pumpkin, winter squash, or with any of these combined with cooked celery or carrot.

Six Servings

Seafood Gumbo

1	bay leaf
¼	teaspoon thyme leaves, crumbled
⅛	teaspoon oregano leaves, crumbled
1	teaspoon salt
¼	teaspoon each white, red and black pepper
1	cup chopped onion
1¼	cups chopped green bell pepper
½	cup chopped celery
6	tablespoons vegetable oil
⅓	cup flour
½	teaspoon minced garlic
2¾	cups seafood stock
8	ounces smoked sausage, cut into ½-inch pieces
8	ounces medium peeled shrimp
6	medium to large oysters in their liquid
12	ounces crab meat

❖ ❖ ❖

Combine the bay leaf, thyme, oregano, salt, white pepper, red pepper and black pepper in a small bowl and set aside. Mix the onion, green pepper and celery in a medium bowl and set aside.

Heat the oil in a large heavy skillet for 5 minutes or just until it begins to smoke. Whisk in the flour. Cook for 2 to 4 minutes or until the roux is dark brown, whisking constantly.

Add half the vegetable mixture. Cook for 1 minute, stirring constantly. Add the remaining vegetable mixture. Cook for 2 minutes, stirring constantly. Stir in the seasonings. Cook for 2 minutes, stirring frequently. Add the garlic. Cook for 1 minute.

Bring the seafood stock to a boil in a 5½-quart stockpot. Add the roux mixture by spoonfuls, stirring well after each addition. Bring to a boil and add the sausage. Cook for 15 minutes, stirring occasionally. Reduce the heat and simmer for 10 minutes longer. Add the shrimp, undrained oysters and crab meat. Bring to a boil over high heat, stirring occasionally; discard the bay leaf. Serve over rice.

Six Servings

Horticulturists in the Conservatory try to garden as naturally as possible, using an organic approach. The staff relies on insecticidal soap and predaceous insects that feed on unwanted spider mites and aphids as part of an integrated pest management program. They also recycle composted leaves, clippings, and plant material into the soil, which was mixed by hand—all 5,200 cubic yards of it, or the equivalent of 385 dump truck loads.

Kentucky Marinated Delight

6	medium tomatoes, blanched, peeled, sliced
1	European cucumber, peeled, seeded, sliced
2	medium purple onions, juilienned
2	packages enoki mushrooms
1	cup tarragon vinegar
2	ounces mustard
2	cups olive oil
1	bunch dill, chopped
	Sugar, salt and pepper to taste
6	heads Bibb lettuce

❖ ❖ ❖

Layer the tomatoes, cucumber slices and onions in a shallow dish. Arrange the mushrooms in 12 bunches over the top.

Combine the vinegar, mustard, olive oil, dill, sugar, salt and pepper in a bowl and mix well. Pour over the layered vegetables. Marinate in the refrigerator for 2 hours.

Place the lettuce leaves on 12 serving plates. Arrange the marinated vegetables over the top.

Twelve Servings

Palms are some of the Conservatory's most prominent tropicals. The gardens contain one of the best collections of Rhapis, or Lady palms, in the United States. The name comes from the Greek word rhapis, which means "needle" and describes the foliage. Other palms include the Fishtail palm, native to Asiatic tropics, and the Phoenix or Pigmy date palm, native to the Canary Islands and Vietnam.

Sautéed Medallions of Pork with Warm Cabbage Salad

Pork
7½	cups pork stock
1½	medium onions, chopped
6	teaspoons thyme
6	bay leaves
1	(1-pound) boneless pork loin
3	tablespoons olive oil
6	shallots, chopped
6	tablespoons madeira

Cabbage
1	cup sauerkraut
½	cup each shredded cabbage and carrot

Salad
1	tablespoon raspberry vinegar
3	tablespoons walnut oil
1½	sprigs tarragon, minced
6	cups mixed fresh salad greens

❖ ❖ ❖

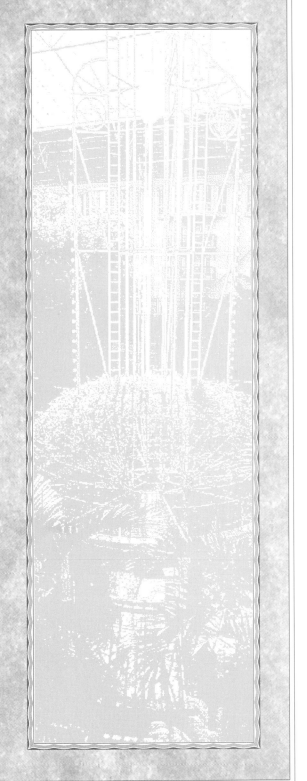

For the pork, combine 1½ cups of the pork stock, onions, thyme and bay leaves in a shallow dish and mix well. Add the pork. Marinate in the refrigerator for 24 hours; drain. Brown the pork on all sides in the heated olive oil in a large skillet. Add the shallots, wine and remaining pork stock, stirring to deglaze the skillet. Simmer for 30 minutes. Cut the pork into medallions. Strain the sauce and return to the skillet. Cook until the mixture lightly coats the back of a spoon.

For the cabbage, sauté the sauerkraut, cabbage and carrot in a nonstick skillet. Add to the reduced sauce and mix well.

For the salad, whisk the vinegar into the walnut oil in a bowl. Add the seasoning mixture. Arrange the salad greens on serving plates. Spoon the cabbage mixture over the greens. Arrange the pork medallions over the cabbage. Drizzle with the dressing and top with cranberries poached in madeira.

Six Servings

Prime Rib Au Jus

1	(8- to 10-pound) prime rib
¼	cup rosemary
½	cup kosher salt
¼	cup pepper
¼	cup soy sauce
¼	cup red wine
2	beef bouillon cubes

❖ ❖ ❖

Place the prime rib in a roasting pan. Rub with rosemary, salt and pepper. Roast at 300 degrees for 2½ to 3 hours. Remove the roast to a serving platter.

Add the soy sauce, wine and bouillon cubes to the pan juices. Add enough water to measure 2 cups liquid. Simmer for 5 minutes, stirring to deglaze the pan. Skim the surface. Serve with the roast.

You may thicken the sauce with a small amount of cornstarch dissolved in cold water or red wine.

Sixteen to Twenty Servings

Baked Smoked Pork Loin

Pork loin

8	ounces stone-ground mustard
4	ounces honey
	Cayenne to taste
2	(3-pound) boneless smoked pork loin
4	small oranges, peeled
1	pound pork caul fat

Cranberry sauce

6	ounces fresh cranberries
½	cup red wine
½	cup pork cooking juices
2	ounces orange marmalade
	Sherry to taste

❖ ❖ ❖

For the pork loin, mix the mustard, honey and cayenne in a bowl. Spread over the top of the pork loin. Cut the oranges into thin slices lengthwise. Arrange half the orange slices over the pork. Cover with half the caul fat. Turn the pork and repeat with the remaining pork ingredients. Wrap in foil and place in a roasting pan. Roast at 350 degrees for 30 minutes. Open the foil and roast for 20 minutes longer, basting frequently.

For the sauce, poach the cranberries in the red wine in a saucepan until they begin to pop. Drain the wine into a saucepan, reserving the cranberries. Drain ½ cup cooking juices from the pork into the saucepan. Add the marmalade and mix well. Cook until reduced to the desired consistency. Season with sherry to taste. Stir in the cranberries.

Serve the pork with the cranberry sauce.

Caul fat is the thin fatty membrane that lines the abdominal cavity and can be purchased through a butcher. It will melt during the cooking process. It may be necessary to soak the membrane in warm salted water to loosen the layers before using. You may also wrap the pork with bacon strips and skewer if preferred.

Six Servings

Poppy Seed Chicken and Spicy Peanut Vanilla Sauce

Peanut Vanilla Sauce
1   vanilla bean, split
4   cups half-and-half
7   tablespoons creamy peanut butter
1   tablespoon crushed red pepper
    Salt to taste
Chicken
6   (6-ounce) boneless skinless chicken breasts
½   cup poppy seeds
    Salt and pepper to taste
½   cup peanut oil
½   cup chopped peanuts
½   cup chopped green onions

❖ ❖ ❖

For the sauce, bring the vanilla bean to a boil in the half-and-half in a saucepan. Cook until reduced by ½. Discard the bean.

Whisk the peanut butter into the saucepan over medium heat; reduce the heat. Add the red pepper and salt. Simmer for 5 minutes. Remove from the heat and keep warm.

For the chicken, rinse the chicken and pat dry. Pound lightly with a meat mallet and sprinkle with the poppy seeds, salt and pepper.

Sauté the chicken in the peanut oil in a skillet until cooked through.

Remove the chicken to serving plates. Spoon the sauce over the top. Sprinkle with the chopped peanuts and green onions.

Six Servings

For a special occasional treat of Chicken Livers, rinse 1 pound of livers and place in a bowl of salted water in the refrigerator overnight. Rinse again and pat dry. Dip the livers in ½ cup milk and coat with a mixture of 1 cup cornmeal and ½ cup flour. Fry in heated oil until golden brown.

Country Vineyard Pheasant

Pheasant
1	pheasant breast
½	ounce sliced country ham
1	grape leaf

Blueberry Sauce
4	ounces fresh or frozen blueberries
¼	cup red wine
	Salt and cayenne to taste
½	tablespoon cornstarch
2	tablespoons madeira

❖ ❖ ❖

For the pheasant, rinse the breast and pat dry. Wrap in the country ham and grape leaf. Place in a baking pan. Roast at 350 degrees for 30 minutes.

For the sauce, bring the blueberries to a boil in the red wine in a saucepan. Add the salt and cayenne.

Blend the cornstarch into the madeira in a small bowl. Stir into the saucepan. Cook until thickened, stirring constantly.

Serve with the pheasant. Serve with wild rice, carrots and snow peas.

One Serving

Admiral's Choice

36	(1-ounce) halibut medallions
	Worcestershire sauce to taste
	Juice of 4 lemons
	Salt and pepper to taste
2⅓	cups flour
10	eggs, beaten
	Butter for sautéing
12	ounces fish velouté (page 45)
1	bunch fresh dill, chopped
2	ounces tomato purée

❖ ❖ ❖

Sprinkle the fish with Worcestershire sauce, lemon juice, salt and pepper. Dip into the flour and eggs. Sauté in butter in a sauté pan until golden brown.

Heat the fish velouté with the dill in a saucepan. Spoon onto the serving plates. Pipe the tomato purée into an ornamental design on the prepared plates.

Arrange 6 fish medallions around the outer edge of each plate. Fill the center with a medley of vegetables sautéed in butter until tender-crisp.

Six Servings

The Opryland Hotel Culinary Institute, a three-year culinary apprentice program, was begun in 1987 to provide the demanding training required to provide top-notch chefs in an industry suffering shortages of skilled culinarians. From 1991 to 1994 the institute was named the best program of its kind in the Southeast by the American Culinary Federation, and in 1995 it was named the best program in the nation. Graduates have taken positions at top restaurants across the nation.

Red Snapper with Basil Beurre Blanc

Basil Beurre Blanc

½   cup white wine
½   cup white vinegar
¼   cup chopped shallots
½   cup heavy cream
8   ounces unsalted butter, cubed
2   tablespoons basil
     Salt and white pepper to taste

Fish

4   (6-ounce) red snapper fillets
     Flour
     Clarified butter for sautéing

For the basil beurre blanc, combine the wine, vinegar and shallots in a saucepan. Cook until reduced by ½. Add the cream. Cook until reduced by ½.

Remove from the heat and whisk in the butter until melted. Strain the mixture into a saucepan. Season with the basil, salt and white pepper. Keep warm.

Coat the fish lightly with flour. Sauté in clarified butter in a saucepan until golden brown. Serve with the sauce.

Four Servings

Southern Velvet

1	small to medium onion, coarsely chopped
2½	pounds fresh or frozen oysters in liquid
1	cup flour
½	cup butter
2	cups clam juice
1	tablespoon lemon juice
2	cups chablis
1	tablespoon brandy
3	bay leaves
	Salt and pepper to taste
2	cups cream
6	ounces cooked lobster meat

Sauté the onion in a nonstick skillet over medium heat until translucent. Add the undrained oysters. Cook until the edges begin to curl. Place the mixture in a blender and process until puréed; set aside.

Blend the flour into the melted butter in a saucepan and cook to form a roux, stirring constantly. Add the clam juice, puréed oysters, lemon juice, wine, brandy, bay leaves, salt and pepper. Simmer for 15 minutes, stirring frequently.

Stir in the cream. Simmer for 5 minutes. Discard the bay leaves or strain if desired and serve immediately. Sprinkle with the lobster meat.

Six Servings

Rice Royale

4	cups cooked rice and wild rice mixture
2¼	cups half-and-half or milk
2	tablespoons minced onion
2	beef bouillon cubes, crushed
8	eggs, beaten
	Nutmeg, salt and white pepper to taste

❖ ❖ ❖

Combine the rice, half-and-half, onion, bouillon cubes, eggs, nutmeg, salt and white pepper in a bowl and mix well. Spoon into a greased baking dish and smooth the top.

Bake at 350 degrees until firm and a wooden inserted in the center pick comes out clean.

Ten Servings

The apprentices in the hotel's culinary training program spend 1,000 hours in the classroom and 6,000 hours of on-the-job training in hotel kitchens. Graduates earn an Associate of Applied Science degree in combination with Volunteer State Community College in Gallatin, Tennessee. The culmination is a final "exam" of two parts: an on-the-spot preparation of a four-course dinner from a set of ingredients in a "mystery box" and the preparation of a showpiece for a special food show.

Wild Mushroom Delight

¼ cup chopped shallots
8 cups fresh mushrooms, cut into quarters
½ cup butter
½ cup red wine
2 ounces dried morel mushrooms
1 (6-ounce) can chanterelle mushrooms
4 cups beef consommé
2 cups heavy cream
   Marjoram, thyme, salt and pepper to taste

❖ ❖ ❖

Sauté the shallots and fresh mushrooms in the butter in a sauté pan over medium heat until tender. Add the wine. Cook until reduced by ½.

Rinse the morels in water well. Drain the chanterelles, reserving the liquid; cut the mushrooms into halves. Add the beef consommé, chanterelles and morels to the sauté pan. Bring to a simmer.

Stir in the cream, marjoram, thyme, salt and pepper. Return to a boil. Serve immediately.

Eight Servings

The horticulturists at the hotel have teamed up with the American Chestnut Foundation in an effort to save the American chestnut, which constituted 25 percent of the hardwood trees in the eastern hills until a blight virtually eliminated it. Chinese chestnuts planted in the Conservatory will be cross-pollinated with American chestnuts planted just outside the Cascades entrance to produce a gene resistant to the blight. Future plans call for including other endangered species such as the Malayan Coconut Palm.

Southern Cheesecake with Strawberry Topping

Crust

10	tablespoons melted butter
6	tablespoons plus 1 teaspoon sugar
1	cup cake crumbs
1	egg
1½	cups flour
1½	tablespoons baking powder
3	tablespoons cinnamon
	Vanilla extract, cinnamon and salt to taste
2½	ounces filberts

Filling

32	ounces cream cheese, softened
1	cup sugar
6	tablespoons plus 1 teaspoon cornstarch
9	ounces sour cream
5	eggs
	Juice of 1 lemon
	Vanilla and salt to taste

Topping

8	ounces fresh strawberries, crushed
¼	cup sugar
3	ounces Grand Marnier

❖ ❖ ❖

Combine the crust ingredients in a bowl and mix well. Press over the bottom and side of a springform pan.

For the filling, beat the cream cheese and sugar in a mixer bowl until smooth. Add the next 6 ingredients and mix well. Spoon into the prepared springform pan. Bake at 300 degrees for 45 minutes. Cool on a wire rack.

For the topping, combine the strawberries, sugar and Grand Marnier in a bowl and mix well.

Place the cheesecake on a serving plate and remove the side of the pan. Spoon the strawberry topping over the cheesecake.

Twelve Servings

Uncle Bud's Bread Pudding

6	slices stale bread
1	teaspoon cinnamon
½	cup seedless raisins
2	tablespoons melted butter
4	eggs
½	cup plus 2 tablespoons sugar
2	cups milk
1	teaspoon vanilla extract

Tear the bread into a 1½-quart baking dish. Sprinkle with the cinnamon and raisins and drizzle with the butter. Place in a 350-degree oven. Toast until light brown.

Combine the eggs, sugar, milk and vanilla in a mixer bowl and mix well. Pour over the toasted bread.

Bake at 350 degrees for 30 minutes or until set. Serve with Melba sauce or rum sauce.

Eight Servings

Jack Daniel's Pie

1	package brownie mix or 1 recipe brownie batter
2½	tablespoons unflavored gelatin
¾	cup water
½	ounce instant coffee
⅓	cup sugar
2	cups milk
1	cup sugar
8	egg yolks
	Vanilla extract to taste
1	egg
1	teaspoon flour
4½	ounces Jack Daniel's whiskey
2	cups plus 2 ounces heavy whipping cream, whipped

Prepare the brownie mix using the package directions. Spread the batter ¼ inch thick over the bottom and side of a pie plate to form the pie shell. Bake in a moderate oven until set.

Soften the gelatin in the water in a saucepan. Stir in the coffee granules and ⅓ cup sugar. Heat until the gelatin, sugar and coffee dissolve completely; do not boil. Remove from the heat and set aside.

Reserve 2 tablespoons of the milk. Combine the remaining milk with 1 cup sugar in a saucepan. Heat over medium heat. Stir in vanilla.

Combine the reserved milk with the egg yolks, egg and flour in a bowl and mix well. Add to the heated milk mixture. Cook until thickened, stirring constantly. Let stand until cool.

Stir in the gelatin mixture and whiskey. Fold in the whipped cream gently. Spoon into the pie shell. Decorate with additional whipped cream and chocolate shavings as desired. Chill until serving time.

Eight Servings

Opryland chefs make Jack Daniel's Pies from a recipe that makes 16 at a time. They use 4 packets of instant coffee granules, 12 ounces of unflavored gelatin, 3 quarts of water, 2 pounds of extra-fine sugar, 12 quarts of whipping cream, 2 quarts of Jack Daniel's whiskey and 16 pie shells.

Goo Goo Pie

2	egg whites
¼	cup sugar
1½	tablespoons plus 1 teaspoon unflavored gelatin
6	tablespoons cold water
2	cups heavy whipping cream
⅔	cup confectioners' sugar
1½	ounces Frangelica or Goo Goo liqueur
2½	ounces caramel topping
2½	ounces peanuts, chopped
½	cup grated milk chocolate
1½	ounces miniature marshmallows
1	baked (10-inch) pie shell
2	cups heavy whipping cream
½	cup confectioners' sugar
1	Goo Goo candy bar
	Dark sprinkles

❖ ❖ ❖

Combine the egg whites and sugar in a double boiler. Heat to 140 degrees on a candy thermometer, beating constantly. Remove from the heat and continue beating until the mixture cools. Soak the gelatin in the water in a saucepan. Heat until the gelatin dissolves. Fold into the meringue.

Whip 2 cups cream with ⅔ cup confectioners' sugar in a mixer bowl until soft peaks form. Add the liqueur. Fold into the meringue with the caramel topping, peanuts, grated chocolate and marshmallows. Spoon into the pie shell. Chill for 20 minutes.

Whip 2 cups cream with ½ cup confectioners' sugar in a mixer bowl until soft peaks form. Spread a portion of the whipped cream over the pie. Pipe the remaining whipped cream into a border around the edge, with a rosette marking each of 8 servings.

Cut the candy bar into 8 pieces and place 1 piece on each rosette. Scatter sprinkles around the edge.

Eight Servings

Blueberry Muffins

6⅔	cups cake flour
¼	cup baking powder
4	teaspoons baking soda
3½	cups sugar
1½	cups vegetable oil
6	eggs
12	ounces sour cream
	Vanilla extract to taste
24	ounces blueberries

Mix the flour, baking powder, baking soda and sugar in a bowl. Add the oil, eggs, sour cream and vanilla and mix well. Fold in the blueberries.

   Spoon into greased and floured muffin cups. Bake at 300 degrees for 20 minutes.

Twenty-Four Muffins

If you have enjoyed a muffin or other confection at the European-style Conservatory Café overlooking the Conservatory, you may want to try some of the delicious recipes on the following pages. You can also find salads, sandwiches, gourmet coffee, iced tea, ice cream, or frozen yogurt at the café. Just look for Major Muffin, who will welcome you at the door.

Cranberry-Orange Muffins

1	orange
1	cup cranberries
⅓	cup sugar
3½	cups bread flour
1½	tablespoons baking powder
	Pinch of baking soda
	Salt to taste
1	cup minus 2 tablespoons sugar
2	eggs
5	tablespoons melted butter
1	cup milk
1½	cups whole cranberries

❖ ❖ ❖

Grind the orange and 1 cup cranberries together. Combine with ⅓ cup sugar in a bowl. Let stand for 30 minutes.

Mix the flour, baking powder, baking soda, salt and 1 cup minus 2 tablespoons sugar in a large bowl. Combine the eggs, butter and milk in a medium bowl and mix well. Add to the flour mixture gradually and mix well.

Stir in the orange and cranberry mixture. Fold in 1½ cups whole cranberries.

Spoon into greased and floured muffin cups. Bake at 375 degrees for 15 to 20 minutes or until muffins test done.

Twenty-four Muffins

Pear and Apple Muffins

1⅓	pounds pears and apples, peeled, chopped
5¼	cups cake flour
1	cup vegetable oil
4	eggs
2¾	cups sugar
3	tablespoons baking powder
2	teaspoons baking soda
12	ounces sour cream

Toss the pears and apples with 2 or 3 tablespoons of the flour in a bowl.

Combine the oil, eggs and sugar in a large bowl and mix well. Add a mixture of the remaining flour, baking powder and baking soda and mix well.

Stir in the sour cream and floured fruit.

Fill greased and floured muffin cups nearly full. Bake at 300 degrees for 25 minutes.

You may bake these in large muffin cups for 40 minutes if preferred.

Twenty-Four Medium Muffins

The shops at the hotel benefit from the services of a manager/buyer who is in constant touch with her contacts in New York and Paris. Although her choices reflect the latest trends on the fashion scene, the prices, unlike those of some hotels' shops, are very competitive. The emphasis is also on a relaxed pace, with a friendly and low-pressure approach, in order to give guests a shopping experience sometimes referred to as another form of entertainment in its own right.

Pumpkin Muffins

6	tablespoons margarine, softened
1	cup sugar
2	ounces pumpkin
2	teaspoons pumpkin pie spice
	Salt to taste
2	or 3 eggs
6	tablespoons milk
2½	cups bread flour
1	tablespoon baking powder
¾	teaspoon baking soda

◈　◈　◈

Cream the margarine and sugar in a mixer bowl until light. Add the pumpkin, spice, salt and beat until smooth.

Beat the eggs and milk in a mixer bowl. Add to the pumpkin mixture and mix until smooth.

Mix the flour, baking powder and baking soda together. Add to the batter and mix well.

Spoon into greased and floured muffin cups. Bake at 375 degrees for 15 to 20 minutes or until muffins test done.

Twelve Muffins

The housekeeping staff at the hotel is proud of their title of state champions in the World Series of Housekeeping. This annual event provides an opportunity for housekeeping employees from hotels across the state to compete for prizes in work-related games. The emphasis in the events, which range from "Attack of the Killer Vacs" to "The Big Bed Make-Off," may be fun, but the skills required are serious indeed.

Chess Pie

½ cup butter, softened
1 cup sugar
¼ cup flour
½ cup evaporated milk
3 egg yolks, slightly beaten
1½ teaspoons vanilla extract
⅛ teaspoon salt
1 unbaked (9-inch) pie shell

❖ ❖ ❖

Cream the butter, sugar and flour in a mixer bowl until light and fluffy. Add the evaporated milk and mix well. Beat in the egg yolks, vanilla and salt.

Spoon into the pie shell. Bake at 325 degrees for 1 hour or until nearly set in the center.

Eight Servings

Chocolate Fudge Pie

½	cup shortening
1⅔	cups sugar
3	eggs
1	tablespoon cornstarch
1	tablespoon flour
⅓	cup melted semisweet chocolate
1	cup milk
1	unbaked pie shell

Cream the shortening and sugar in a mixer bowl until light and fluffy. Beat in the eggs.

Mix the cornstarch and flour in a bowl. Add to the creamed mixture alternately with the chocolate, mixing well after each addition. Add the milk gradually.

Spoon into the pie shell. Bake at 325 degrees for 45 minutes or until set. Cool completely.

Eight Servings

Fresh Peach Pie

1   cup cake crumbs
1   unbaked (9-inch) pie shell
4   or 5 medium peaches, peeled, sliced
2   eggs
2   tablespoons sugar
6   tablespoons milk
2   tablespoons heavy cream
     Vanilla extract to taste
     Salt to taste

Sprinkle the cake crumbs in the pie shell. Layer the peach slices over the crumbs.

Beat the eggs and sugar in a mixer bowl. Mix the milk, cream, vanilla and salt in a small bowl. Add to the egg mixture and mix well. Pour over the peaches.

Bake at 350 degrees for 45 to 50 minutes or until set. Cool to room temperature. Glaze with apricot preserves if desired.

Eight Servings

Opryland Hotel's Special Events Wedding Department offers a one-stop wedding shop, providing everything from the rehearsal through the flowers, music, minister, photographer, and reception, and even planning the honeymoon. Louise Mandrell, William Lee Golden, and James Garner's daughter are some of the more-famous newlyweds. The saddest event was probably that of the brave bride who went ahead and entertained her guests at a large reception even though the groom didn't show up.

Pecan Pie

½	cup butter, softened
½	cup sugar
3	large eggs
1	cup light corn syrup
1	teaspoon vanilla extract
⅛	teaspoon salt
1½	cups pecans
1	unbaked (9-inch) pie shell

Cream the butter and sugar in a large mixer bowl until light and fluffy. Beat in the eggs 1 at a time. Add the corn syrup, vanilla and salt. Stir in the pecans. Spoon into the pie shell.

Bake at 450 degrees for 10 minutes. Reduce the oven temperature to 350 degrees. Bake for 30 minutes longer or until a knife inserted in the center comes out clean.

Eight Servings

Sacher Torte

Torte

9	tablespoons butter
¾	cup plus 1 tablespoon sugar
6¼	ounces chocolate
	Vanilla extract to taste
7	egg yolks
8	egg whites
1¼	cups flour
1	cup apricot jam

Icing

5¼	ounces chocolate, chopped
6	tablespoons sugar
9	tablespoons warm water

For the torte, cream the butter and half the sugar in a mixer bowl until light and fluffy. Melt the chocolate with the vanilla in a double boiler over hot water. Add to the creamed mixture and mix well. Beat in the egg yolks gradually.

Beat the egg whites in a mixer bowl until stiff peaks form. Fold in the remaining sugar. Fold in the flour and chocolate mixture.

Spoon into a floured tube pan. Bake at 350 degrees until the torte tests done. Remove to a wire rack to cool.

Slice horizontally into 3 layers. Spread the apricot jam between the layers.

For the icing, combine the chocolate with the sugar and warm water in a bowl. Beat until the chocolate dissolves and the mixture is of the desired consistency. Spread over the torte.

Twelve Servings

Weddings at Opryland Hotel are truly magic and give the hotel's pastry chef a chance to shine, creating wedding cakes that are truly works of art. Using a mouthwatering Italian cream cake as the foundation, the chef spreads icing, spins sugar, and shapes hundreds of tiny flowers tied with sugar-satin ribbons, and then may sculpt a pair of white chocolate turtledoves to perch on top. The amazing fact is that he may be called on to do as many as eight in one day!

Mounds Cake

Cake
5	cups cake flour
2½	cups sugar
8	teaspoons baking powder
1	tablespoon baking soda
¾	cup baking cocoa
13	tablespoons butter, softened
14	tablespoons melted shortening
4	eggs
2¼	cups milk
½	cup each water and sugar

Ganache
1½	cups heavy cream
19	ounces semisweet chocolate, chopped

Coconut Topping
2½	cups coconut
¼	cup light corn syrup
½	cup cream of coconut

❖ ❖ ❖

For the cake, mix the flour, 2½ cups sugar, baking powder, baking soda and cocoa in a large bowl. Add the butter and shortening. Beat for 5 to 7 minutes. Beat the eggs with the milk in a mixer bowl. Add to the batter ⅓ at a time, beating well after each addition and scraping the side of the bowl.

Spoon into 3 greased and floured cake pans. Bake at 350 degrees until the layers test done. Remove to a wire rack to cool.

Boil the water and ½ cup sugar in a saucepan until the sugar dissolves. Sprinkle over the layers.

For the ganache, bring the cream to a boil in a saucepan and remove from the heat. Stir in the chocolate until melted; cool. Spread between the layers and pipe a border around the top.

Mix the topping ingredients in a bowl. Add a small amount of water if needed for the desired consistency. Spread over the top of the cake.

Sixteen Servings

THE CASCADES

The magic of the sight and
sound of water is the theme of the Cascades
garden at Opryland Hotel. This two-acre area, home to
approximately 8,200 plants representing 449 species, is crowned
by a one-acre skylight and features three waterfalls ranging in height
from 23 to 30 feet. They pour from the top of a 40-foot mountain into a
12,500-square-foot lake below. The spellbinding wonder that is billed as
"Dancing Water"™ is a breathtaking display of cascades, laser beams and
live music, programmed and synchronized by a custom computer.

A prominent feature of the Cascades is the Promenade, an elevated
walkway that winds through the mountain, over the waterfalls, and
under the towering palms. Stairways lead down to the lake and the
fountain. The Cascades Lobby, located adjacent to the garden, is
the main hub for guests arriving and departing from the Hotel.
This entrance features twin swimming pools over the
very busy portico where uniformed doormen
assist with transportation.

THE CASCADES

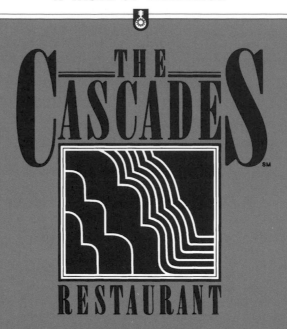

THE CASCADES RESTAURANT

The Cascades Restaurant offers a unique dining experience, featuring American items as well as the California-Pacific flavors suggested by the tropical setting. The restaurant is composed of several small "islands" separated by rushing streams, bluffs, and waterfalls, and provides ringside seats for the "Dancing Waters" laser and fountain show. The Cascades' specially-designed showcase kitchen allows guests to watch chefs prepare a wide assortment of dishes.

In addition to the restaurant, a revolving lounge in the center of the lake showcases the Lobby Bar on the lower level of the Cascades. This lower level is also home to the Fitness Center, The Children's Shoppe, Savannah's, women's apparel and accessories and Accents, which offers that special and hard to find gift to take home.

Pacific Crab Cakes

Crab Cakes

¼   cup heavy cream
      Chopped lemon grass
1   pound Dungeness crab meat
¼   cup Panko bread crumbs
2   tablespoons coarsely chopped cilantro
1   teaspoon finely chopped shallots
2   egg yolks
¼   cup mayonnaise
      Salt, cayenne and freshly ground black pepper to taste
      Olive oil for sautéing

Lime Sauce

¼   cup each sweet rice wine and white wine
1   piece lemon grass, chopped
      Juice of 1 lime
¼   cup heavy cream
1   cup butter, chopped
1   ounce wasabi paste
Black Bean Relish (page 114)

❖ ❖ ❖

For the crab cakes, combine the cream and lemon grass in a saucepan. Cook until reduced to 2 tablespoons. Mix with the crab meat, bread crumbs, cilantro, shallots, egg yolks, mayonnaise, salt, cayenne and black pepper in a bowl.

Shape into 2-ounce cakes and coat with additional bread crumbs. Sauté in olive oil in a sauté pan until cooked through.

For the lime sauce, combine the wines, lemon grass and lime juice in a saucepan. Cook until syrupy, stirring frequently. Add the cream. Cook until reduced to the desired consistency.

Reduce the heat to low. Whisk in the butter, maintaining the sauce between 100 and 140 degrees. Whisk in wasabi paste.

To assemble, spoon Black Bean Relish onto serving plates. Place the crab cakes on the prepared plates. Drizzle the lime sauce around the edge. Garnish with a sprig of cilantro.

Four Servings

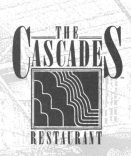

Even though you can leave the cooking to the famous chefs at the Cascades Restaurant, you can enjoy watching them do it in the state-of-the-art showcase kitchen. If you prefer, you can relax in a gazebo or under an umbrella beside dancing waters to enjoy a meal of either American fare or fare with the slightly exotic accent of the Pacific Rim. The recipes on the following pages showcase some of those special dishes.

You can enjoy the dancing waters in the Cascades at any time of the day, since the 22-foot fountain in the Cascades performs a continuous series of water movements from 8:00 a.m. until 11:00 p.m., but you won't want to miss the special performances accompanied by live music at seven o'clock and nine o'clock daily.

Black Bean Relish

8	ounces cooked black beans, rinsed
¼	cup each rice vinegar and olive oil
¼	cup each finely chopped red onion, red bell pepper and yellow bell pepper
2	tablespoons each chopped cilantro, chives and green onions

❖ ❖ ❖

For the relish, combine the beans, vinegar, olive oil, onion, bell peppers, cilantro, chives and green onions in a bowl and mix well. Chill until serving time.

Four Servings

Cucumber Soup

2   European cucumbers
16   ounces plain yogurt
5   ounces sour cream
     Lemon juice to taste
1   tablespoon instant chicken bouillon
2   tablespoons chopped dill
     Salt and pepper to taste

❖ ❖ ❖

Peel and seed the cucumbers. Purée in a food processor. Add the yogurt, sour cream, lemon juice, chicken bouillon, dill, salt and pepper. Process until smooth. Season with salt and pepper.
    Chill until serving time. Serve cold.

Five Servings

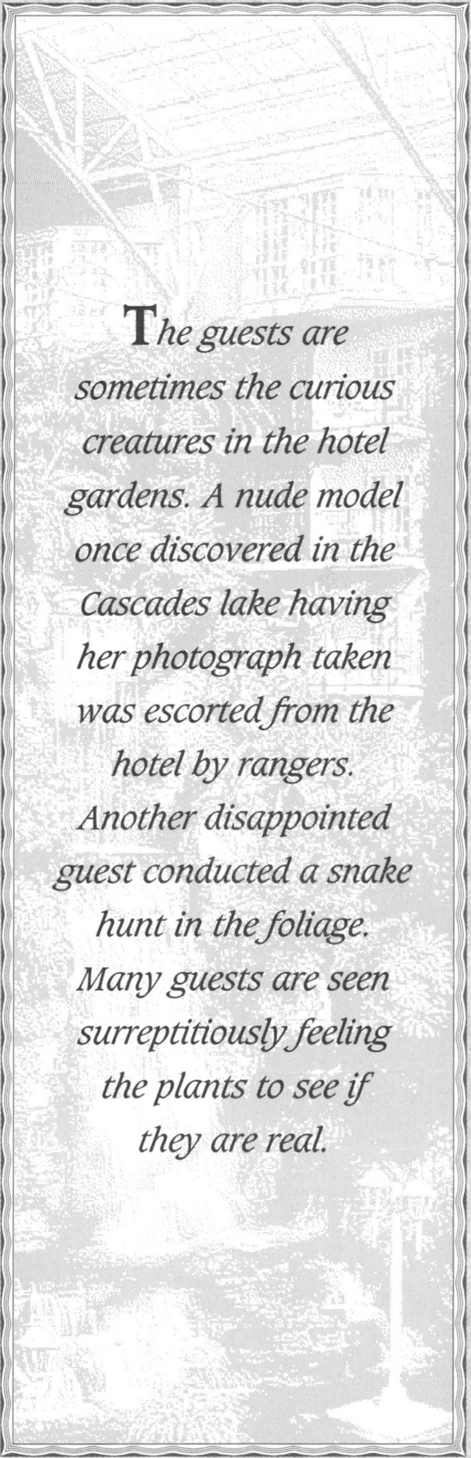

The guests are sometimes the curious creatures in the hotel gardens. A nude model once discovered in the Cascades lake having her photograph taken was escorted from the hotel by rangers. Another disappointed guest conducted a snake hunt in the foliage. Many guests are seen surreptitiously feeling the plants to see if they are real.

Each week landscaping crews put on their waders to retrieve the coins tossed into the hotel's fountains. The unchlorinated well water is good for the plants, but it also covers the coins with calcium and other mineral deposits. Local banks will count the coins, but only after they have been cleaned. For five years they were cleaned by hand, but the hotel finally had to buy an $8,000 machine to "launder" the money. Proceeds are contributed to an employee relief fund for ten months of the year and the remainder to Nashville's Crusade for Children.

Garlic Cream Soup

2	cups chopped garlic
6	cups sliced onions
¼	cup olive oil
6	cups chicken stock
	Bouquet garni of parsley, thyme and bay leaf
½	loaf dried bread, crumbled
2	cups heavy cream
	Salt and pepper to taste

Cook the garlic and onions in the olive oil in a saucepan over very low heat for 30 minutes or until golden brown, stirring occasionally.

Add the chicken stock, bouquet garni and bread. Simmer for 30 minutes. Discard the bouquet garni. Process in a food processor until smooth.

Combine the puréed mixture with the cream, salt and pepper in a saucepan. Bring just to a simmer. Serve with French bread.

Eight Servings

Tomato Basil Soup

1	cup chopped onion
1	cup chopped celery
2	tablespoons margarine
1	clove of garlic, crushed
1½	cups chopped fresh basil
8	cups chicken stock or water
1	tablespoon salt
1	(6-ounce) can tomato paste
¼	teaspoon crushed dillweed or tarragon

❖ ❖ ❖

Sauté the onion and celery in the margarine in a saucepan until tender.

Add the garlic, basil, stock and salt. Simmer for 1½ hours.

Stir in the tomato paste and dill. Cook until heated through.

Eight Servings

Iceberg Slaw

½	cup mayonnaise
2	cups Italian salad dressing
6	tablespoons pickle relish
2	tablespoons cumin
2	tablespoons chili powder
4	cups shredded iceberg lettuce
1	cup shredded red cabbage
1	cup shredded carrots
	Salt to taste

❖ ❖ ❖

Combine the mayonnaise, salad dressing and relish in a bowl. Add the cumin and chili powder and mix well.

Add the lettuce, cabbage, carrots and salt; mix lightly. Chill for 30 minutes.

Ten Servings

Rest your fears that the Opryland Hotel complex has grown too vast. To address that problem in comfort and style, the hotel provides both on- and off-property bus transportation by the largest privately-owned bus transportation system in the state of Tennessee. In one year, vehicles ranging in size from vans to 51-seat motor coaches will log about 1,000,000 miles and consume 23,000 gallons of diesel fuel.

Pasta Salad

1	pound uncooked tri-color pasta
1	cup broccoli florets
1	cup cauliflowerets
½	cup grated carrot
6	ounces black olives
2	tablespoons chopped garlic
2	cups (about) mayonnaise
¼	cup ranch salad dressing
	Salt and white pepper to taste

Cook the pasta al dente using the package directions; rinse with cold water and drain.

Combine the pasta with the broccoli, cauliflower, carrot, olives and garlic in a large bowl.

Add the mayonnaise and salad dressing. Season with salt and white pepper.

Eight Servings

Fusilli with Fresh Tomato Salad

¾	cup virgin olive oil
¼	cup balsamic or malt vinegar
1	tablespoon chopped garlic
¾	teaspoon salt
1	tablespoon freshly ground pepper
4	medium tomatoes, coarsely chopped
½	cup chopped mixed fresh parsley, basil, oregano and marjoram
½	cup sliced black olives
¼	cup sliced green onions
12	ounces fusilli, cooked, drained

❖ ❖ ❖

Combine the olive oil, vinegar, garlic, salt and pepper in a bowl and mix well. Add the tomatoes, fresh herbs, olives and green onions. Mix gently.

Add the pasta and toss lightly to coat well. Chill until serving time.

Six Servings

Opryland Hotel's Springhouse Golf Club features an award-winning Sunday brunch for hotel guests and the dining public. The brunch is served from 9:30 to 2:30 in the glass-enclosed dining room on the mezzanine level of the 43,000-square-foot clubhouse, giving diners a spectacular view of the golf course. Look for the shuttle at the Cascades Lobby every half-hour for the five-minute ride to the clubhouse.

Sweet-and-Sour Vinaigrette

2	onions, coarsely chopped
2	tablespoons celery seeds
¾	cup paprika
2	cups white vinegar
1½	cups sugar
¼	cup salt
¼	cup salad oil

❖ ❖ ❖

Process the onions, celery seeds and paprika in a blender until smooth.

Bring the vinegar, sugar and salt to a rolling boil in a saucepan. Remove from the heat. Stir in the oil.

Combine the vinegar mixture with the onion mixture in a bowl and mix well. Store, covered, in the refrigerator.

The Cascades serves this dressing with their Asian-style spinach salad with mushrooms, water chestnuts and sprouts.

Six Cups

Herbed Lamb Loin

1	(6- to 8-pound) lamb loin
	Fresh marjoram, oregano, thyme, rosemary
	and parsley
½	cup chopped onion
½	cup chopped celery
1	bunch tarragon, chopped
1	bunch mint, chopped
¼	cup flour
½	cup chopped onion
½	cup chopped celery
1	cup red wine
	Salt and pepper to taste
½	cup chopped onion
1	cup chopped mushrooms
1	clove of garlic, chopped
2	tablespoons butter
1	egg
1½	cups chopped pecans
1½	bunches watercress, chopped
1	cup butter, chopped

❖ ❖ ❖

Bone the lamb, reserving the bones and nerves and leaving the lamb in 1 piece. Remove and finely chop the excess meat on the belly flap. Remove and reserve the stems from the fresh herbs.

To make the stock, combine the lamb bones and nerves, reserved herb stems, ½ cup onion, ½ cup celery and half the tarragon and mint in a saucepan. Add enough water to cover the bones well. Simmer for 2 hours.

Remove the nerves from the saucepan. Brown in a skillet. Stir in the flour. Cook until brown. Add ½ cup onion and ½ cup celery. Add the wine, stirring to deglaze. Stir in the lamb stock with the remaining tarragon and mint. Simmer for 1 hour. Season with salt and pepper.

Sauté ½ cup onion, mushrooms and garlic in 2 tablespoons butter in a skillet. Combine with the chopped meat, lamb stock, egg, pecans, watercress, herb leaves, salt and pepper in a bowl and mix well. Stuff into the lamb; roll to enclose the filling and tie securely. Wrap with foil.

Place in a roasting pan. Roast at 350 degrees for 25 minutes. Remove the foil. Roast for 20 minutes longer, basting occasionally.

Strain the sauce through a cheesecloth into a saucepan. Cook over low heat until heated through. Remove from the heat. Add 1 cup butter gradually, mixing well. Serve with the lamb. Serve with Poached Pears (page 140), Parmesan Potatoes (page 137) and sautéed vegetables.

Eight Servings

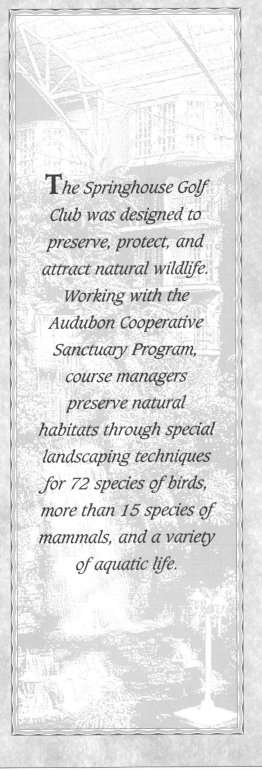

The Springhouse Golf Club was designed to preserve, protect, and attract natural wildlife. Working with the Audubon Cooperative Sanctuary Program, course managers preserve natural habitats through special landscaping techniques for 72 species of birds, more than 15 species of mammals, and a variety of aquatic life.

The BellSouth Senior Classic PGA Golf Tournament has become an annual event at the hotel's Springhouse Golf Club. It attracts some of the world's best-known golfers to play on the links-style course designed by Larry Nelson with course architect Jeff Brauer. The design of the course and the bleachers on many of the holes makes it ideal for tournament play.

Prime New York Strip Steak with Tomato Onion Chutney

1	cup sugar
¼	cup white wine vinegar
½	teaspoon mustard seeds
1½	cups chopped onions
2⅔	cups coarsely chopped tomatoes
1	teaspoon Dijon mustard
1	teaspoon minced garlic
2	teaspoons minced crystallized ginger
1	teaspoon finely chopped parsley
1	teaspoon finely chopped chives
1	teaspoon finely chopped thyme
½	teaspoon Madras curry powder
4	(12-ounce) prime New York strip steaks

❖ ❖ ❖

Combine the sugar, vinegar and mustard seeds in a saucepan. Cook over low heat until reduced to a syrup. Add the onions and cook until translucent.

Stir in the tomatoes, mustard, garlic, ginger, parsley, chives, thyme and curry powder. Cook until of the desired consistency; do not allow to become too dark.

Grill the steaks until done to taste. Serve with the tomato onion chutney.

Four Servings

Pecan-Crusted Pork Loin with Sesame Ginger Aioli

Pork

2	cups Panko bread crumbs or other bread crumbs
1	cup chopped pecans
8	(3- to 4-ounce) pieces pork loin
	Salt and pepper to taste
2	cups flour
3	eggs, beaten
	Vegetable oil for browning

Sesame Ginger Aioli

1	cup mayonnaise
2	tablespoons sesame oil
1	tablespoon rice wine vinegar
2	tablespoons soy sauce
1	tablespoon Dijon mustard
¼	cup roasted garlic purée
2	tablespoons minced fresh ginger

❖ ❖ ❖

For the pork, mix the bread crumbs and pecans in a shallow dish. Trim the pork, discarding the fat and silver skin. Pound lightly. Season with salt and pepper. Coat with the flour. Dip in the eggs. Place in the pecan mixture, pressing lightly to coat well.

Brown on all sides in oil in a skillet over medium-hot heat. Remove to a roasting pan. Roast at 350 degrees until cooked through.

For the sesame ginger aioli, combine the mayonnaise, oil, vinegar, soy sauce, mustard, garlic and ginger in a bowl and mix well. Adjust flavors to suit your taste.

Serve the pork topped with the aioli. Garnish with tomato concasse.

Four Servings

The Country Radio Seminar's 25th anniversary celebration at Opryland Hotel was one of three events in 1995 to win a Gala Award from Special Events magazine. The event required, among other things, 6,000 yards of black Spandex; 1,000 pounds of glass blocks for 237 hand-assembled centerpieces containing 200 gallons of water, 4,800 inches of white neon tubing, and 600 hot pink tulips; 13,650 square feet of black draping; 4 custom-built fog machines and 2,700 pounds of dry ice to create a fogged floor; and 24,000 inches of silver lamé.

Plantation-Style Pork

1	(4-pound) pork loin
2	cups bread crumbs
3	cups chopped peanuts
1	bunch parsley, chopped
4	stems rosemary, chopped
1	clove of garlic, chopped
	Salt and pepper to taste
1	tablespoon dry English mustard
½	cup water
1	tablespoon walnut oil
1	(8-ounce) jar chutney

Trim the pork and cut into 3-ounce medallions. Mix the bread crumbs, peanuts, parsley, rosemary, garlic, salt and pepper in a bowl and set aside.

Blend the mustard, water and oil in a bowl. Spread lightly on one side of each pork medallion. Top with a thin layer of chutney. Coat on both sides with the bread crumb mixture.

Sauté in a lightly buttered sauté pan over medium-high heat until golden brown on both sides.

Eight Servings

Char Siu-Style Breast of Chicken with Corn Fritters

Chicken
1	cup hoisin sauce
½	cup soy sauce
½	cup honey
1	tablespoon garlic purée
1	tablespoon minced ginger
½	cup packed brown sugar
1	tablespoon annatto seeds
1	teaspoon Chinese five-spice powder
4	(7-ounce) chicken breasts

Corn Fritters
16	ounces fresh or frozen corn kernels
1	tablespoon minced garlic
¼	cup chopped scallions
2	eggs, beaten
¼	to ½ cup flour
	Salt and pepper to taste

❖ ❖ ❖

For the chicken, mix the hoisin sauce, soy sauce, honey, garlic, ginger, brown sugar, annatto seeds and five-spice powder in a saucepan. Simmer for 30 minutes. Strain the sauce and adjust the flavor to suit your taste.

Rinse the chicken and pat dry. Grill on a lightly oiled grill until cooked through, basting with the sauce.

For the corn fritters, combine the corn, garlic, scallions, eggs, flour, salt and pepper in a bowl and mix well. Spoon in small dollops onto a griddle oiled with olive oil until golden brown on both sides.

Serve the chicken on jasmine rice with corn fritters and a garnish of chives.

Four Servings

Stuffed Chicken Breasts

3½	cups crumbled corn bread
2½	cups (or more) dry bread crumbs
3	eggs
5	cups chicken or turkey broth
½	cup melted butter
1	small onion, finely chopped
½	cup finely chopped celery
½	cup chopped parsley
½	teaspoon (scant) sage
½	teaspoon (scant) poultry seasoning
	Salt and pepper to taste
6	to 8 boneless chicken breasts
	Melted butter

❖ ❖ ❖

Combine the crumbled corn bread, bread crumbs, eggs, chicken broth, butter, onion, celery, parsley, sage, poultry seasoning, salt and pepper in a bowl and mix well. Add additional bread crumbs if needed to bind.

Rinse the chicken and pat dry. Season with salt and pepper. Spoon the stuffing onto the chicken and fold or roll to enclose the stuffing.

Arrange skin side up in a baking pan. Drizzle with butter. Bake at 350 to 375 degrees for 25 to 30 minutes or until a meat thermometer registers 145 degrees.

You may add chopped chestnuts to the stuffing if desired.

Six to Eight Servings

Chicken Casserole

½   cup butter
½   cup flour
1   cup milk
1   cup chicken stock
¼   cup chopped onion
½   cup sliced mushrooms
¼   cup butter
4   cups chopped cooked chicken
½   cup sherry
      Salt and pepper to taste
½   cup bread crumbs
1   tablespoon paprika
2   tablespoons melted butter

❖ ❖ ❖

Melt ½ cup butter in a saucepan and blend in the flour. Cook over low heat for 5 minutes. Stir in the milk and chicken stock. Cook until thickened, stirring constantly; set aside.

Sauté the onion and mushrooms in ¼ cup butter in a saucepan until tender. Add the chicken. Sauté for 5 minutes. Stir in the sherry. Cook for 5 minutes or until the liquid has nearly evaporated.

Add the sauce and mix well. Season with salt and pepper. Spoon into a baking dish. Top with bread crumbs and paprika; drizzle with melted butter. Bake at 350 degrees for 1 hour.

Eight Servings

Opryland Hotel is talkin' trash. In the first year of its recycling program in 1991, the hotel collected 18 tons of computer paper and 600,000 aluminum cans, as well as office paper, corrugated cardboard, and kitchen oils. The program was expanded to include glass, scrap metal, soap, and plastic. Estimates indicate that the first year's efforts saved almost 3,000 trees.

Orange Roughy Opryland

Fish
1 pound mushrooms, sliced
3 tablespoons chopped shallots
3 tablespoons butter
6 (6-ounce) orange roughy fillets
6 (5-inch) squares puff pastry
1 egg, beaten

Velouté
2 tablespoons flour
2 tablespoons butter
2 cups fish stock
Salt to taste
½ cup cream

❖ ❖ ❖

For the fish, sauté the mushrooms and shallots in the butter in a skillet until tender.

Place each fish fillet on 1 pastry square. Top with the mushroom mixture. Wrap the pastry to enclose the fish. Brush with the egg.

Place in a baking pan. Bake at 375 degrees for 20 minutes.

For the velouté, blend the flour into the butter in a saucepan. Cook until golden brown to form a roux, stirring constantly. Stir in the fish stock gradually. Cook until thickened, stirring constantly. Cook for 15 to 20 minutes. Season with salt. Strain into another saucepan. Stir in the cream. Serve with the fish.

Six Servings

Snappy Snapper

3	tablespoons flour
3	tablespoons melted butter
1½	cups fish stock
½	cup cream
¼	cup Jack Daniel's whiskey
	Salt and white pepper to taste
6	(6-ounce) red snapper fillets
1½	cups flour
½	cup butter
6	fresh dill sprigs

❖ ❖ ❖

Blend 3 tablespoons flour into 3 tablespoons butter in a saucepan. Cook until golden brown, stirring constantly. Stir in the fish stock gradually. Cook until thickened, stirring constantly. Simmer for 15 minutes. Stir in the cream and whiskey. Season with salt and white pepper.

Coat the fish with a mixture of 1½ cups flour, salt and white pepper. Brown on both sides in ½ cup butter in a sauté pan.

Place the fish on serving plates. Top with the whiskey sauce. Garnish with sprigs of dill.

Six Servings

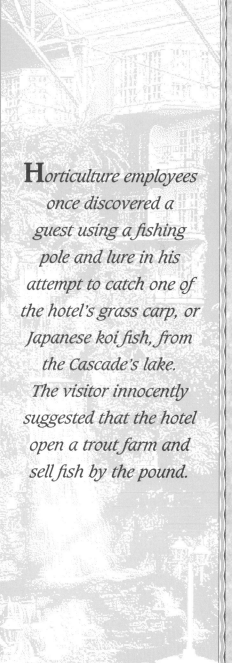

Horticulture employees once discovered a guest using a fishing pole and lure in his attempt to catch one of the hotel's grass carp, or Japanese koi fish, from the Cascade's lake. The visitor innocently suggested that the hotel open a trout farm and sell fish by the pound.

Shrimp and Scallop Pasta

½	cup chopped yellow onion
½	cup chopped green bell pepper
1	clove of garlic, minced
¼	cup butter
2	tablespoons Italian seasoning
¼	cup red wine
¼	cup flour
1	cup tomato juice
4	teaspoons sugar
	Salt and pepper to taste
10	(16- to 20-count) shrimp, peeled, deveined
10	medium sea scallops
2	tablespoons butter
8	ounces spaghetti, cooked, drained

❖ ❖ ❖

Sauté the onion, green pepper and garlic in ¼ cup butter in a saucepan until tender. Stir in the Italian seasoning and wine. Cook until reduced by ½.

Stir in the flour. Add the tomato juice. Cook until thickened, stirring constantly. Simmer for 30 minutes. Add additional flour if needed for the desired consistency. Season with sugar, salt and pepper.

Sauté the shrimp and scallops in 2 tablespoons butter in a sauté pan until cooked through. Add to the sauce. Simmer for 2 minutes. Serve over the pasta.

Two Servings

Opryland Hotel offers several vacation packages that take advantage of special events at the hotel and allow guests to sample other attractions such as the Opryland Theme-park and the General Jackson showboat. Favorite packages include "A Country Christmas," "Easter Eggstravaganza," "Spring into Summer," "Firecracker Vacation," and "End O' Summer Vacation."

Treasure of the Sea

1	teaspoon chopped shallot
½	teaspoon minced garlic
½	teaspoon butter
8	shrimp
8	scallops
8	mushrooms, cut into quarters, blanched
1	cup sherry
2	cups heavy cream
	Salt and pepper to taste

❖ ❖ ❖

Sauté the shallot and garlic in the butter in a nonstick sauté pan. Add the shrimp, scallops and mushrooms. Sauté for several minutes.

Add the sherry, stirring to deglaze the sauté pan. Cook until reduced by ¾. Stir in the cream. Cook until thickened or reduced by ½. Season with salt and pepper to taste. Serve in puff pastry shells or over rice.

Two Servings

Vegetarian Pasta with Balsamic Vinaigrette

Balsamic Vinaigrette
½	cup balsamic vinegar
½	cup sherry vinegar
2	cups olive oil
½	cup chopped shallots
	Chopped parsley, marjoram, thyme and rosemary
	Salt and freshly ground pepper to taste
8	tomatoes
2	portobello mushrooms

Pasta
1	cup sliced shiitake mushrooms
2	tablespoons olive oil
½	cup pine nuts, lightly toasted
½	cup coarsely chopped basil
1	pound pasta, cooked al dente
½	cup freshly shaved Parmesan cheese

❖ ❖ ❖

For the vinaigrette, combine the vinegars, olive oil, shallots, fresh herbs, salt and pepper in a bowl and mix well. Cut the tomatoes into halves and squeeze out the seeds. Add to the vinaigrette with the mushrooms. Marinate in the refrigerator overnight.

Drain the tomatoes and mushrooms, reserving the vinaigrette. Grill the tomatoes and mushrooms on a heated grill just until they begin to char or the color begins to change. Season with salt and pepper. Chop the tomatoes and return to the vinaigrette. Chill until serving time. Set the mushrooms aside.

For the pasta, sauté the mushrooms in the olive oil in a saucepan. Add 2 cups of the vinaigrette, pine nuts and basil and mix well. Toss the mixture with the pasta in a large bowl. Spoon into large serving bowls. Slice the reserved portobello mushrooms. Sprinkle the mushrooms and cheese over the pasta.

Four Servings

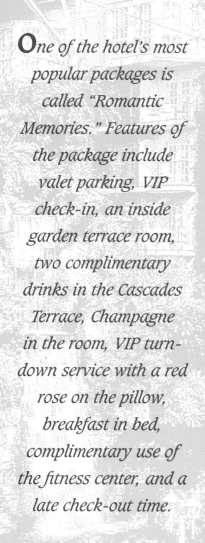

One of the hotel's most popular packages is called "Romantic Memories." Features of the package include valet parking, VIP check-in, an inside garden terrace room, two complimentary drinks in the Cascades Terrace, Champagne in the room, VIP turn-down service with a red rose on the pillow, breakfast in bed, complimentary use of the fitness center, and a late check-out time.

Vegetarian Strudel

2	or 3 cloves of garlic, minced
1	large onion, julienned
1	carrot, julienned
¼	head cabbage, julienned
6	mushrooms, sliced
2	tablespoons sesame oil
1	teaspoon ground ginger
	Crushed red pepper flakes to taste
2	tablespoons peanut butter
	Soy sauce to taste
½	cup plum sauce
1	pound vegetable protein chicken, chopped
½	cup cornstarch
1	sheet puff pastry
1	egg, beaten

❖ ❖ ❖

Sauté the garlic, onion, carrot, cabbage and mushrooms in the heated sesame oil in a large sauté pan until tender-crisp. Add the ginger and red pepper flakes.

Stir in the peanut butter, soy sauce, plum sauce and vegetable protein chicken. Sprinkle with the cornstarch and stir to mix well. Cool to room temperature; chill in the refrigerator.

Spoon down the center of the puff pastry; roll to enclose completely. Cut several steam vents.

Place on a baking sheet. Brush with egg. Bake at 350 degrees until golden brown.

Four Servings

Potato Dumplings

2   **pounds potatoes, peeled, chopped**
      Salt to taste
1   **cup (or more) flour**
2   **eggs, lightly beaten**
      Nutmeg and pepper to taste
30   **herbed croutons**

❖ ❖ ❖

Cook the potatoes in salted water in a saucepan until tender; drain. Mash the potatoes. Chill overnight.

Combine the potatoes with 1 cup flour, eggs, nutmeg, salt and pepper in a bowl and mix well. Add additional flour 1 spoonful at a time if needed to form a dough.

Shape into dumplings with floured hands, pressing several croutons into the center of each dumpling.

Drop into salted boiling water in a saucepan. Simmer for 10 to 15 minutes or until cooked through.

Serve with German Sauerbraten (page 34).

Ten Servings

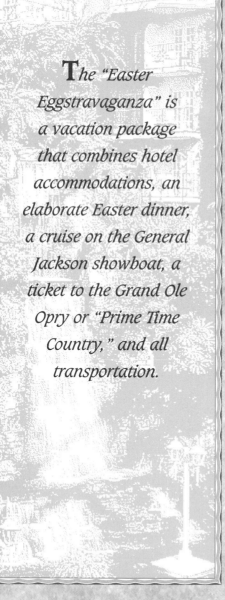

The *"Easter Eggstravaganza" is a vacation package that combines hotel accommodations, an elaborate Easter dinner, a cruise on the General Jackson showboat, a ticket to the Grand Ole Opry or "Prime Time Country," and all transportation.*

Parmesan Potatoes

12	baking potatoes
1	onion, chopped
	Salt and pepper to taste
1	cup butter, sliced
6	ounces grated Parmesan cheese

❖ ❖ ❖

Place the potato slices on buttered foil. Sprinkle with the onion, salt and pepper. Dot with butter. Seal the foil.

Bake at 350 degrees for 30 to 40 minutes or until the potatoes are tender. Open the foil. Sprinkle with the cheese. Broil until golden brown.

Twelve Servings

Potato Quiche

3   cups shredded potatoes
⅓   cup minced onion
6   eggs
4   cups half-and-half
½   cup beef stock
       Nutmeg and white pepper to taste

❖ ❖ ❖

Sauté the potatoes and onion in a nonstick skillet for 2 minutes.
    Whisk the eggs in a large bowl. Add the potato mixture, half-and-half, beef stock, nutmeg and white pepper, whisking to mix well.
    Spoon into a buttered baking dish. Bake at 325 degrees for 20 minutes.

Six Servings

The hotel's Gold Platter Award *distinguishes it as one of the top 20 convention-catering operations in the world, a tribute to the 32 different hotel departments that are usually involved in the planning process. Factors include budget, menu selection, room arrangement, decorations, meal times, and entertainment. Details go into a 7-foot-wide book that gives an overview of the events of the day.*

Roman-Style Gnocchi

5   cups milk
5   ounces butter, melted
¼   teaspoon nutmeg
½   teaspoon salt
1¾   to 2¼ cups semolina or yellow cornmeal
2   egg yolks
1   cup grated Parmesan cheese

❖ ❖ ❖

Combine the milk, 1¾ ounces of the butter, nutmeg and salt in a saucepan. Bring to a boil. Sprinkle the semolina into the saucepan and stir to mix well. Cook over low heat for 15 minutes, stirring constantly. Remove from the heat. Stir in the egg yolks and 7 tablespoons of the cheese.

Spread ¾ to 1 inch deep in a buttered shallow pan. Cool to room temperature. Cut into circles 1¾ to 2 inches in diameter. Arrange in a buttered baking dish with the edges overlapping.

Sprinkle with the remaining cheese and drizzle with the remaining butter. Bake at 425 degrees for 10 to 15 minutes or until a golden yellow crust is formed.

Ten Servings

Poached Pears

4	cups white wine
1	cup water
1	cup sugar
1	bunch mint leaves
1	ounce mint extract
4	pears
8	radiccio leaves
	Pecan halves

❖ ❖ ❖

Combine the wine, water and sugar in a saucepan. Bring to a boil. Add the mint and mint extract.

Peel the pears, cut into halves and discard the cores. Add to the poaching liquid. Simmer until tender.

Arrange radiccio leaves on serving plates. Place 1 pear half on each plate; sprinkle with pecans. Serve with Herbed Lamb Loin (page 122).

Eight Servings

Apple Cake

Topping
8	ounces or 1 cup packed almond paste
1	cup sugar
¾	cup butter, softened
½	teaspoon vanilla extract
3½	cups flour

Cake
6	eggs
1	cup sugar
½	teaspoon salt
4⅔	to 4¾ cups flour
½	teaspoon baking powder
¾	cup orange juice
1	cup vegetable oil
4	apples, sliced
	Cinnamon-sugar

❖ ❖ ❖

For the topping, mix the almond paste, sugar, butter and vanilla in a bowl until smooth. Add the flour and mix lightly until crumbly.

For the cake, combine the eggs, sugar and salt in a mixer bowl and beat until thick and pale yellow. Add the flour and baking powder; mix until smooth. Add the orange juice. Stir in the oil gradually.

Layer half the cake batter and half the apples in a greased and floured tube pan. Sprinkle with the cinnamon-sugar. Add the remaining cake batter and apples and sprinkle with the topping.

Bake at 350 degrees for 45 minutes or until the cake tests done. Cool in the pan on a wire rack.

Sixteen Servings

Opryland Hotel's ice sculptures are individual works of art, created by the hotel's own chefs. Sculptures begin as 300-pound blocks of ice and turn out as anything from animals such as horses or eagles to company logos. The original designs are initially roughed out with a chainsaw. A chisel is used for detail, a propane torch smooths the ice and makes it crystal clear, and a router blade provides the fine lines. The snow produced by the router blade is then packed back into the lines for contrast.

Mandarin Chocolate Brownie Tart

Crust

1	cup flour
¼	cup packed light brown sugar
1	ounce unsweetened chocolate, grated
1	tablespoon milk
1	teaspoon vanilla extract
½	cup butter, chopped

Filling

3	ounces each unsweetened and semisweet chocolate
½	cup butter, softened
3	large eggs
1½	cups sugar
2	teaspoons vanilla extract
½	cup chopped macadamia nuts
¾	cup flour

Topping

2	ounces semisweet chocolate
¼	cup butter
1	teaspoon vegetable oil
2	ounces white chocolate, melted

❖ ❖ ❖

For the crust, combine the flour, brown sugar and chocolate in a bowl. Add the milk and vanilla and mix well. Cut in the butter. Press evenly into an 11-inch tart pan. Chill in the refrigerator.

For the filling, melt the chocolate in a double boiler. Add the butter and mix until smooth. Beat the eggs 1 at a time into the sugar in a mixer bowl. Mix in the vanilla and macadamia nuts. Add the chocolate mixture and mix well. Mix in the flour gradually. Pour into the crust. Bake at 350 degrees for 20 minutes. Cool on a wire rack.

For the topping, heat the first 3 ingredients in a double boiler, stirring to mix well. Spread evenly over the tart. Drizzle with the white chocolate and swirl with a spatula to marbleize.

Eight to Twelve Servings

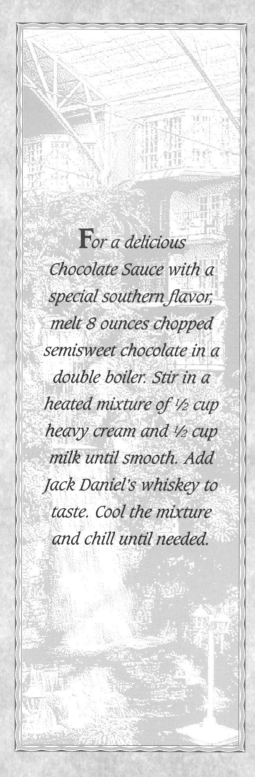

For a delicious Chocolate Sauce with a special southern flavor, melt 8 ounces chopped semisweet chocolate in a double boiler. Stir in a heated mixture of ½ cup heavy cream and ½ cup milk until smooth. Add Jack Daniel's whiskey to taste. Cool the mixture and chill until needed.

Coconut Pies

4	egg yolks
⅔	cup sugar
⅓	cup cornstarch
	Vanilla extract to taste
3	cups milk
½	cup sugar
1	cup toasted flaked coconut
⅓	cup creme of coconut
2	baked (9-inch) pie shells

❖ ❖ ❖

Combine the egg yolks, ⅔ cup sugar, cornstarch and vanilla in a bowl and mix well.

Combine the milk and ½ cup sugar in a saucepan. Bring to a boil. Stir in the cornstarch mixture. Cook until thickened, stirring constantly.

Mix the coconut and creme of coconut in a bowl. Add to the custard and mix well. Spoon into the pie shells.

Twelve Servings

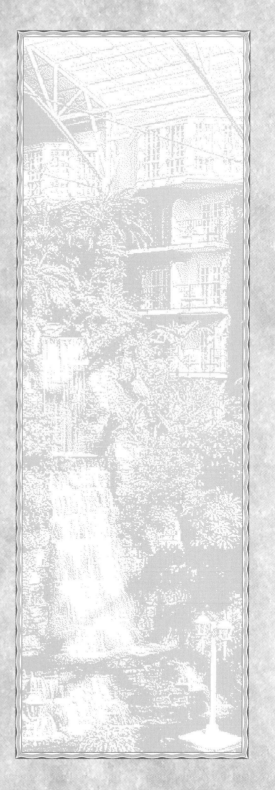

Traditional Key Lime Pie

7	ounces sweetened condensed milk
⅓	cup sugar
10	tablespoons key lime juice
7	egg yolks
1	(9-inch) pie shell
7	egg whites
1½	tablespoons plus ½ teaspoon cream of tartar
¾	cup sugar

❖ ❖ ❖

Combine the condensed milk and ⅓ cup sugar in a bowl and mix well. Add the lime juice and egg yolks and mix just until blended.

Spoon into the pie shell. Bake at 350 degrees for 20 minutes or just until set.

Beat the egg whites with the cream of tartar in a mixer bowl until foamy. Add ¾ cup sugar gradually, beating until stiff but not dry peaks form.

Spread over the pie, sealing to the edge. Bake for 15 minutes longer or broil just until golden brown.

Eight Servings

THE DELTA

At Opryland Hotel's Delta,
you can step out of your everyday life and
deep into the subtropical world of the Mississippi
River delta—an amazing four-and-one-half-acre indoor garden
with a flowing river more than a quarter mile in length, complete
with five flatboats that can carry 25 passengers each—all crowned by a
glass roof that soars to a height of 150 feet. No matter what the weather
is outside, here the temperature and humidity are always pleasant and you
are never far from a cool beverage, a memorable meal, or a hotel room.

The garden environment is enhanced with 370 trees, palms that are
between 20 and 40 feet tall, and thousands of smaller plants. The signature
plants are the sabal palm, the southern magnolias, and the gardenias.
There are, in addition, black olive and huge mahogany trees. And, yes,
that really is Spanish moss trailing from the branches.
With the completion of the Delta, the hotel now boasts 2,883 guest rooms,
and 600,000 square feet of meeting and exhibit facilities. This includes
seven meeting and board rooms on the upper levels of the
Delta island which feature beautiful
views of the area.

THE DELTA

The focal point of the Delta is the 20,000 square foot ante-bellum-style mansion, which houses the 400 seat gourmet restaurant, Beauregard's. In addition, the Delta Court offers a variety of quick-service restaurants complemented by deli

carts, vendors, and shops offering homemade candy, beignets, and ice cream. Some of the food opportunities are Tennessee Wok, Beignet Cafe, Sweet Treats, Sweet Surrender, Delta Burger, and Delta Deli. Amid all the wonderful food choices, live music from the lounges lends a steady beat to the atmosphere. There is exciting shopping available from antique collectibles at Riverview Gallery to stylish

casual clothing and accessories at Amelia's and Willow Creek. Visitors can take home items from the Delta's distinctive country shop, Bushels & Baskets or even a living bonsai or windchime from The Green Leaf. Keynotes showcases and sells country music, even the oldies

and goodies and the Delta Gift and Sundries Shoppe gives you a wide spectrum of gift opportunities, including sundries and newspapers.

Catfish Pâté

½   medium onion, chopped
12   ounces cream cheese, softened
2   to 3 teaspoons chopped fresh dill
2   teaspoons (or more) freshly squeezed lemon juice
1   teaspoon Tabasco sauce
1   pound hickory-smoked catfish, flaked

❖ ❖ ❖

Sauté the onion lightly in a nonstick skillet.

Combine the onion, cream cheese, dill, lemon juice and Tabasco sauce in a food processor container. Process until mixed. Fold in the catfish.

Serve on a bed of greens with basil vinaigrette and toast points.

Two to Three Cups

Beauregard's

The flavors of the bounty from the waters of the Mississippi and the Gulf combine in the cuisine found at Beauregard's. The recipes in this chapter include some of those delightful dishes with the true southern accent of the Delta. You will enjoy preparing these delicious dishes at home as you recall your interlude at the Delta at Opryland Hotel.

Cajun Coulis for Shrimp Cocktail

5	red peppers, roasted, peeled, seeded
10	Roma tomatoes, cut into halves, seeded
3	tablespoons horseradish
	Juice of 1 lemon
	Juice of 1 lime
5	tablespoons minced garlic
3	tablespoons Cajun seasoning
½	cup honey
4	sprigs of fresh thyme
	Salt and pepper to taste
½	cup Worcestershire sauce
½	tablespoon prepared mustard

❖ ❖ ❖

Combine the peppers, tomatoes, horseradish, lemon juice, lime juice, garlic, Cajun seasoning, honey, thyme, salt, pepper, Worcestershire sauce and mustard in a blender container. Process until smooth.

Serve with marinated grilled shrimp and herbed oil.

Two to Three Cups

Escargot Strudel

1	pound butter
5	(70-count) cans escargot, drained, rinsed
2	cups minced shallots
2	cups minced garlic
	Salt and pepper to taste
1¼	cups white wine
2½	pounds spinach, rinsed, drained
5	packages frozen phyllo dough, thawed
4	pounds butter, melted
3	pounds feta cheese, crumbled

❖ ❖ ❖

Melt 1 pound butter in a large skillet. Add the escargot, shallots, garlic, salt and pepper. Sauté for 5 minutes. Add the wine. Cook for several minutes, stirring to deglaze the skillet. Add the spinach. Cook until the spinach is wilted. Let cool.

Brush 1 sheet of the dough with some of the melted butter. Top with another sheet of dough and spread with butter. Repeat until there are 4 layers. Cut into halves crosswise. Remove 14 to 16 escargot from the sautéed mixture with a slotted spoon. Arrange 7 to 8 escargot 1½ inches from narrow edge of cut dough pieces. Top with the spinach and cheese. Fold in the sides. Roll from the narrow edge, brushing with additional butter if needed and tucking in the dough. Repeat with the remaining ingredients.

Fifty Servings

The Delta gardens boast several magnolia trees weighing up to 16,000 pounds, with trunks 14 inches in diameter. People sometimes ask where you go to buy a 40-foot-tall magnolia tree. The horticulture manager, in certain circumstances, has been known to knock on someone's door and offer to buy a tree right out of the homeowner's yard, and several were bought that way. "It's tricky moving a tree that size, but it obviously can be done. It takes special equipment and a BIG truck," he says.

Oysters Bienville

6	tablespoons butter
1½	cups deveined peeled shrimp
1	cup chopped scallions
1½	cups finely chopped mushrooms
¾	cup flour
1½	cups chicken stock
6	tablespoons white wine
6	egg yolks
1	cup whipping cream
8	ounces bacon, crisp-fried, crumbled
2	tablespoons Worcestershire sauce
1	tablespoon finely chopped fresh parsley
3	dozen oysters, shucked, drained
	Freshly grated Parmesan cheese

❖ ❖ ❖

Melt the butter in a sauté pan. Add the shrimp, scallions and mushrooms. Sauté for 10 minutes or until the shrimp turn pink. Sprinkle with the flour. Cook for 10 minutes, stirring constantly. Remove from the heat.

Add the chicken stock and wine, stirring until smooth. Add the egg yolks, whipping cream and bacon. Return to the heat. Cook until thickened, stirring constantly. Stir in the Worcestershire sauce and parsley.

Arrange the oysters in a single layer in a baking pan. Pour the shrimp mixture over the oysters. Bake at 350 degrees for 10 to 12 minutes or until the oysters curl.

Four to Six Servings

The construction of the Delta added 140,750 square feet of dedicated meeting rooms and pre-function space to the hotel, including a gigantic 55,269-square-foot ballroom that seats 5,500. That ballroom complements the hotel's other three major ballrooms that have between 18,000 and 30,000 square feet.

French Onion Soup

6	medium onions, thinly sliced
3	tablespoons butter
¼	cup dry white wine
6	cups beef broth
	Salt and pepper to taste
½	cup shredded Swiss cheese
	Sliced French bread, broken into 1-inch chunks
2	tablespoons grated Swiss cheese

❖ ❖ ❖

Sauté the onions in the butter in a large kettle over medium heat for 7 to 8 minutes or until lightly browned. Stir in the wine and broth. Simmer, covered, for 30 minutes. Season with salt and pepper.

Place 6 ovenproof ceramic soup bowls or soup plates on a baking sheet. Pour in the soup, dividing the onions evenly. Stir in the shredded cheese. Place 2 to 3 pieces of bread in each soup bowl. Sprinkle with the grated cheese when the bread floats to the surface.

Bake at 325 degrees for 20 minutes. Broil just until the cheese is brown.

Six Servings

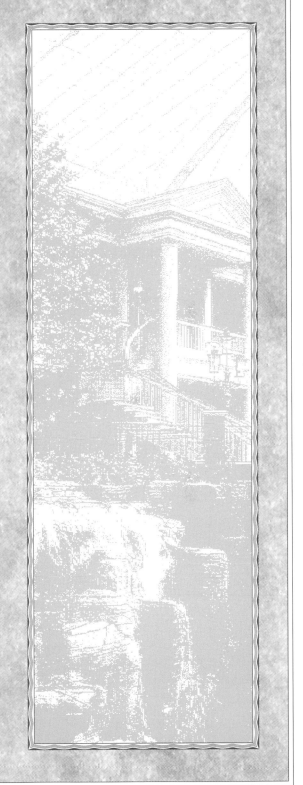

Wild Rice Soup

1	cup uncooked wild rice
5	cups water
1	cup butter
1	cup chopped onion
1	cup chopped celery
1	cup diced carrots
½	cup slivered almonds
½	cup flour
½	cup diced ham
1	gallon chicken stock
	Salt and pepper to taste
1	cup heavy cream

❖ ❖ ❖

Cook the rice in the water in a saucepan. Drain, reserving 1 cup liquid.

Melt the butter in a stockpot. Add the onion, celery, carrots and almonds. Sauté until tender. Add the flour. Cook for 5 minutes; do not brown. Add the ham, chicken stock and reserved liquid. Bring to a boil.

Add the rice; reduce the heat. Simmer for 10 minutes. Season with salt and pepper. Add the cream. Simmer just until heated through.

Twenty-Four Servings

Bayou Crab Soup

1	teaspoon minced onion
6	tablespoons butter
¾	cup flour
4	cups milk, scalded
¼	cup bourbon
8	ounces snow crab meat
¼	cup clam juice
1	teaspoon lemon juice
1	teaspoon Dijon mustard
	Tabasco sauce to taste

❖ ❖ ❖

Sauté the onion in the butter in a saucepan until translucent. Stir in the flour. Cook for 3 or 4 minutes, stirring constantly.

Stir in the milk. Bring to a boil, stirring constantly. Reduce the heat.

Heat the bourbon in a small saucepan until reduced. Add to the soup with the crab meat, clam juice, lemon juice, mustard and Tabasco sauce; mix well. Simmer for 30 minutes.

Six Servings

On one day alone at the hotel, delegates to the Chevrolet convention and car show consumed 800 dozen eggs, 3,000 pounds of beef, 1,500 lobsters, 2,000 pounds of chicken, 1,000 pounds of duck, 4,000 pounds of fresh vegetables, 2,000 pounds of fresh fruit, 55,000 rolls and pastries, and 2,000 pounds of Viennese strudel. It involved 300 waiters and bartenders, 75 housemen for setup, 70 stewards for cleanup, and 35 chefs. Fifteen audio-visual specialists provided sound and lighting for a Reba McEntire concert that followed dinner.

Delta Turtle Soup

1	pound clarified butter
1¼	cups (about) flour
¼	cup butter
2	to 2¼ pounds turtle meat, chopped
1¼	to 1½ cups chopped celery
2	cups chopped onions
½	tablespoon chopped garlic, or to taste
1	to 2 bay leaves
½	tablespoon tomato paste
6¾	to 7 cups veal stock
1	tablespoon fresh oregano, or to taste
½	tablespoon fresh thyme, or to taste
¼	tablespoon chopped fresh parsley
¼	tablespoon freshly ground pepper, or to taste
	Salt to taste
½	tablespoon freshly squeezed lemon juice

❖ ❖ ❖

To make a roux, heat the clarified butter in a saucepan or skillet until almost smoking. Stir in the flour. Cook until the flour is browned, stirring constantly.

Heat ¼ cup butter in a skillet, tilting to cover the surface. Add the turtle meat. Cook over high heat until browned. Add the celery, onions, garlic and bay leaves. Cook until the onion is translucent. Add the tomato paste and roux. Simmer for 10 minutes.

Add the veal stock 1 cup at a time, stirring constantly. Cook until thickened, stirring constantly. Add the oregano, thyme, parsley, pepper, salt and lemon juice. Remove the bay leaves before serving.

Six to Ten Servings

Beauregard's Fruit Plate

1	cantaloupe
1	kiwifruit
3	Bibb lettuce leaves
1	small cluster of grapes about the size of a peach
1	cup mixed fruit
5	strawberries, cut into quarters
10	blueberries
5	blackberries
3	whole strawberries

❖ ❖ ❖

Cut the cantaloupe on the bias; trim the bottom so that it stands up high on 1 side. Reserve the remaining cantaloupe for another use. Cut off each end of the kiwifruit. Crown each half; do not peel.

Place the lettuce on 1 edge of the plate. Place the cantaloupe on the lettuce. Place the grapes at the base of the cantaloupe, angled toward the opposite side of the plate. Fill the cantaloupe cavity with the mixed fruit, allowing it to cascade over the grapes. Place kiwifruit pieces crown side up on opposite sides of the cantaloupe. Top with the quartered strawberries, blueberries and blackberries. Fill in any empty spaces with the whole strawberries.

One Serving

Beauregard's Romaine and Stilton salad is served with strawberries, Spicy Pecans, and Strawberry Vinaigrette. For the vinaigrette, heat 1 cup of ripe strawberries, then mash and strain. Combine the liquid with 1 cup red wine vinegar, 3 cups salad oil and 1 or 2 minced shallots and mix well. Store in the refrigerator. For the spicy pecans, drizzle pecan halves with melted butter, Worcestershire sauce and maple syrup. Sprinkle with barbecue sauce, cayenne, salt and black pepper. Toast in a moderate oven for 15 minutes.

Zesty Black-Eyed Peas

2   (16-ounce) cans black-eyed peas, rinsed, drained
1   cup chopped celery
1   green bell pepper, chopped
1   large tomato, peeled, chopped
1   clove of garlic, minced
2   green onions, sliced
1   (4-ounce) jar diced pimento, drained
1   (8-ounce) bottle Italian salad dressing
    Lettuce leaves
3   slices bacon, crisp-fried, crumbled
3   green onions, thinly sliced

❖ ❖ ❖

Combine the peas, celery, green pepper, tomato, garlic, 2 green onions, pimento and salad dressing in a large bowl, tossing gently. Chill, covered, for 8 hours or longer, stirring occasionally. Drain well. Spoon into a lettuce-lined bowl. Sprinkle with the bacon and 3 green onions.

Eight Servings

When the decision was made to expand the hotel by the addition of the Delta, the hotel was virtually at maximum capacity, with more than 3.5 million advance room nights already on the books and an occupancy rate averaging better than 85 percent.

Shrimp Salad

1	pound bay shrimp
1	cup chopped celery
1	cup sliced green onions
2	teaspoons chopped fresh dill
1½	cups mayonnaise
	Salt and pepper to taste

❖ ❖ ❖

Drain the shrimp well. Combine with the celery, green onions, dill, mayonnaise, salt and pepper in a bowl and mix well. Chill until serving time. Serve on lettuce-lined plates.

Four Servings

Seafood Salad

1	pound crab meat, drained
8	ounces lobster claws and knuckles, drained
1	pound bay shrimp, drained
1	cup chopped celery
1	cup sliced green onions
1	tablespoon chopped fresh dill
1	cup mayonnaise
	Salt and pepper to taste

❖ ❖ ❖

Combine the crab meat, lobster meat, shrimp, celery, green onions, dill, mayonnaise, salt and pepper in a large bowl and mix gently. Chill, covered, until serving time.

Six to Eight Servings

House Dressing

1	rib celery
½	onion, coarsely chopped
3	cloves of garlic
4	anchovies
2	cups mayonnaise
1	tablespoon oregano
	White pepper to taste

❖ ❖ ❖

Combine the celery, onion, garlic and anchovies in a blender and process until smooth. Combine with the mayonnaise, oregano and white pepper in a bowl and mix well. Store in the refrigerator for up to 7 days.

Twenty Servings

Thousand Island Dressing

3	cups mayonnaise
1	cup chili sauce
1	tablespoon lemon juice
2	tablespoons chopped pimento
2	tablespoons chopped green bell pepper
3	tablespoons chopped yellow onion
	Salt and pepper to taste

❖ ❖ ❖

Combine the mayonnaise, chili sauce and lemon juice in a bowl and mix well. Add the pimento, green pepper and onion and mix well. Season with salt and white pepper. Store, covered, in the refrigerator.

Twenty-Four Servings

Prime Entrecôte Aux Poivre

1   (12-ounce) New York steak
     Green peppercorn paste
     Sauterne, heated
     Clarified butter
¼   cup brandy
     Minced shallots to taste
     Minced garlic to taste
1   tablespoon coarsely chopped tomato
     Chopped fines herbes to taste
¼   cup veal glacé
2   tablespoons heavy cream
1   teaspoon butter

❖ ❖ ❖

Rub the steak with the peppercorn paste. Place in a skillet with a small amount of sauterne and clarified butter. Sear until golden brown on both sides.

Remove the steak to a roasting pan. Roast at 350 degrees until done to taste.

Add the brandy to the skillet, stirring to deglaze. Add the shallots, garlic, tomato and fines herbes. Stir in the veal glacé. Cook until reduced by ½. Add the cream. Cook until reduced to the desired consistency. Fold in the butter. Adjust the seasoning. Serve with the steak.

One Serving

To make Veal Glacé, skim the fat from veal stock and place in a saucepan. Cook at a slow rolling boil until reduced by ½. Strain through a cloth.

Veal Scaloppine

4	(2- to 3-ounce) pieces of veal
	Flour
	Clarified butter
½	cup white vinegar
½	cup white wine
2	tablespoons chopped shallots
½	cup heavy cream
1	cup unsalted butter, cut into pieces
	Lemon juice to taste
	Salt and white pepper to taste

❖ ❖ ❖

Coat the veal lightly with flour. Sauté in clarified butter in a skillet; keep warm.

Combine the vinegar, wine and shallots in a saucepan. Cook until the liquid is reduced by ½. Add the cream. Cook until reduced by ½. Remove from the heat.

Whisk in the butter gradually. Strain through a sieve. Add the lemon juice, salt and pepper. Serve over the veal.

Four Servings

Opryland Hotel is the perfect choice for a New Year's Eve celebration, with live music to suit everyone's taste. Choose from a gala evening with traditional music and a gourmet Champagne dinner or celebrate with the hottest of rising country music stars at a party that ends with a midnight breakfast— all climaxed with thousands of balloons dropping from the ceiling.

Pork Medallions

Sauce Vinaigrette

1½	cups pork or chicken stock
¼	cup cider vinegar
2	tablespoons sugar
	Salt, cayenne and black pepper to taste
2	ounces cornstarch

Pork

8	(3-ounce) pork medallions
½	cup flour
	Salt and pepper to taste
2	tablespoons clarified butter
½	cup chopped apple
1	cup pearl onions
¼	cup apple brandy

❖ ❖ ❖

For the sauce, combine the pork stock, vinegar, sugar, salt, cayenne and black pepper in a stockpot. Simmer for 30 to 40 minutes or until of the desired consistency, stirring occasionally. Blend the cornstarch with a small amount of water. Stir into the stock mixture. Cook until thickened, stirring constantly. Set aside.

For the pork, coat the pork medallions with a mixture of the flour, salt and pepper. Sauté in the butter in a sauté pan until golden brown. Add the apple and onions and sauté for several minutes.

Add the brandy, stirring to deglaze the skillet. Stir in the sauce. Cook for 2 minutes. Serve on heated plates with parslied potatoes and mixed fresh vegetables.

Four Servings

Cumin-Wrapped Roast Pork Loin with Papaya Chutney

1   tablespoon dried cumin
1   teaspoon salt
1   teaspoon cracked pepper
1   teaspoon marjoram leaves
1   teaspoon paprika
1   teaspoon basil leaves
1   (4- to 5-pound) pork loin
     Vegetable oil
     Papaya Chutney (page 165)

❖ ❖ ❖

Mix the cumin, salt, pepper, marjoram leaves, paprika and basil leaves in a bowl and set aside. Sear the pork loin in oil in a stockpot until browned. Rub the pork loin with the cumin mixture. Place in a roasting pan. Roast at 350 degrees for 1½ hours.

Slice the pork loin. Top each serving with 2 to 3 ounces of papaya chutney.

Ten to Fifteen Servings

Papaya Chutney

⅓	cup water
⅓	cup cider vinegar
⅓	cup sugar
1	tablespoon lime juice
1	tablespoon minced onion
3	papayas, peeled, seeded, chopped
2	tablespoons raisins
4	whole cloves
1	cinnamon stick
1	tablespoon curry powder
½	teaspoon ground ginger
½	teaspoon ground cardamom
⅛	teaspoon red pepper flakes
¼	teaspoon ground nutmeg
1	tablespoon diced green bell pepper
1	tablespoon diced red bell pepper

❖ ❖ ❖

Bring the water, vinegar, sugar, lime juice and onion to a boil in a saucepan; reduce the heat. Simmer until the liquid is reduced by ½.

Add the papayas, raisins, cloves, cinnamon stick, curry powder, ginger, cardamom, red pepper flakes and nutmeg. Simmer over low heat for 1 hour, adding a small amount of water if needed.

Add the bell peppers. Simmer for 10 minutes. Cool to room temperature. Discard the cinnamon stick.

Four Cups

Opryland Hotel offers a winter wonderland for those after-the-holiday blahs. Throughout the winter the hotel keeps the fireplaces blazing to welcome guests to their "Country Winter Celebration," with special vacation packages to warm the heart even when the weather outside is frightful.

Roast Pork Roulade

10	to 15 sun-dried tomatoes
¾	cup shredded smoked Gouda cheese
¾	cup shredded smoked Cheddar cheese
1	(5- to 8-pound) center-cut pork loin
1	pound pork forcemeat, ground twice
3	pounds fresh spinach, blanched, drained, finely chopped
	Salt and pepper to taste
	Rosemary to taste
	Olive oil

❖ ❖ ❖

Soak the tomatoes in a small amount of water until reconstituted. Drain well and cut into julienne strips. Mix the tomatoes, Gouda cheese and Cheddar cheese in a bowl. Stuff the mixture into a sausage casing or roll tightly in plastic wrap. Freeze for several hours or until solid.

Butterfly the pork loin by slicing it horizontally to but not through one side. Open the sides and pound to an even thickness.

Mix the forcemeat with the spinach in a large bowl. Spread over the pork loin.

Remove the cheese roll from the casing or plastic wrap. Place at one end of the pork loin. Roll to enclose the cheese mixture, securing with string or wooden picks. Season with salt, pepper, rosemary and olive oil. Let stand, wrapped in plastic wrap, for 1 hour.

Remove the pork loin from the plastic; rewrap in foil. Place in a roasting pan. Roast at 350 degrees for 55 to 65 minutes or until a meat thermometer registers 140 degrees.

Remove from the oven. Let stand for 10 to 15 minutes. Slice on the bias with a sharp knife.

Twelve to Twenty Servings

Chicken Breast Orleans

4	(8-ounce) boneless skinless chicken breasts
4	ounces shrimp
4	ounces scallops
1	to 2 tablespoons chopped onion, or to taste
2	tablespoons butter
	Chopped dill, parsley and cilantro to taste
	Salt and pepper to taste
¼	cup Worcestershire sauce
8	ounces ground chicken
4	eggs
6	cups heavy cream

❖ ❖ ❖

Rinse the chicken breasts and pat dry. Pound flat between sheets of waxed paper.

Sauté the shrimp, scallops and onion in the butter in a skillet or sauté pan. Add the dill, parsley, cilantro, salt, pepper and Worcestershire sauce and stir gently. Let cool.

Combine the ground chicken, shrimp mixture, eggs and cream in a large bowl. Spread over the flattened chicken. Fold to enclose the filling. Place in a roasting pan.

Roast at 350 degrees for 45 to 60 minutes or until the chicken is cooked through.

Four Servings

The perfect gift for the golfer in your life is the "Nashville Golf Escape." The package offers two nights' room accommodations at Opryland Hotel; three 18-hole rounds of golf at either the Springhouse Golf Club or one of three other area golf clubs; a commemorative Springhouse Golf Club bag tag; one dozen golf balls; complimentary range balls, tees, ball markers, a divot ball, and a souvenir BellSouth Senior Classic Cup.

Grilled Chicken with Curried Rice

Chicken
6   (6-ounce) chicken breasts
1   cup Italian salad dressing

Curried Rice
½   cup mayonnaise
2   tablespoons grainy mustard
2   tablespoons curry powder
1   tablespoon honey
3   cups cooked rice
2   cups chopped celery
1   cup seedless red grapes
1   apple, chopped
¼   cup chopped green onions

❖ ❖ ❖

Rinse the chicken and pat dry. Pour the salad dressing over the chicken in a large bowl. Marinate, covered, in the refrigerator for 1 hour.

For the curried rice, combine the mayonnaise, mustard, curry powder and honey in a medium bowl and mix well. Add the rice, celery, grapes, apple and green onions and mix gently. Chill in the refrigerator.

Remove the chicken from the marinade. Grill over hot coals until cooked through. Let stand for several minutes before slicing thinly. Serve with the curried rice.

Six Servings

Plantation Chicken

5	(8-ounce) chicken breasts
	Salt and pepper to taste
1	to 2 tablespoons melted butter
2	tablespoons chopped shallots
2	tablespoons butter
2	tablespoons brown sugar
1	cup white wine
1	ounce peanut butter
4	cups chicken stock
½	tablespoon lime juice
½	cup sherry
5	tablespoons cornstarch

❖ ❖ ❖

Rinse the chicken and pat dry. Season with salt and pepper. Brush with the melted butter. Place in a baking pan. Bake at 425 degrees for 20 minutes or until cooked through.

Sauté the shallots in 2 tablespoons butter in a skillet. Add the brown sugar, white wine, peanut butter, chicken stock, lime juice and sherry. Simmer until reduced by ½, stirring frequently. Season with additional salt and pepper.

Blend the cornstarch with a small amount of cold water. Stir into the skillet. Bring to a boil, stirring constantly; reduce the heat. Simmer until of the desired consistency. Serve over the chicken.

Five Servings

Housekeeping employees are always ready to provide hospitality for the guests at Opryland, but some of the requests are more unusual than others. A good example is the request for material to tar and feather a convention leader. Eager to please, housekeepers stopped by the hotel kitchen for a gallon of molasses and disassembled a couple of feather pillows for the event.

Black Grouper in Potato Crust with Tomato Beurre Blanc

Fish
24   (4-ounce) pieces grouper
     Salt and pepper to taste
6   to 8 medium potatoes, peeled, thinly sliced
     Olive oil

Tomato Beurre Blanc
5   ounces shallots, peeled, finely chopped
½   cup white wine
1   cup white wine vinegar
½   cup coarsely chopped tomato
½   cup tomato juice
2   pounds butter, cut into 1-inch cubes
     Salt and pepper to taste

❖ ❖ ❖

For the fish, season the grouper with salt and pepper. Dry the potatoes and brush lightly with the olive oil. Place the grouper in a lightly oiled baking pan. Cover on all sides with the potato slices. Bake at 400 degrees for 10 to 12 minutes or until the grouper flakes easily and the potatoes are golden brown.

For the tomato beurre blanc, combine the shallots, wine and vinegar in a heavy saucepan. Simmer until the liquid is reduced by 90 percent. Add the tomato and tomato juice. Whisk in the butter over high heat. Season with salt and pepper.

Spoon a small amount of the sauce onto each plate. Top with the grouper and potatoes. Garnish with sour cream, fresh vegetable rounds and dill.

Twenty-Four Servings

Riverboat Fillet of Flounder

36	(2-ounce) flounder fillets
½	cup lemon juice
	Worcestershire sauce to taste
	Salt and pepper to taste
1½	cups flour
2	cups butter
3	bananas
	Lemon juice
12	ounces whole almonds without skins
1	cup butter
1	bunch white grapes, seeded
1	bunch blue grapes, seeded

❖ ❖ ❖

Season the flounder with the lemon juice, Worcestershire sauce, salt and pepper. Dip in the flour. Sauté in 2 cups butter in a skillet until the fish flakes easily. Roll up fillets and place 3 fillets on each plate; keep warm.

Slice the bananas and dip in lemon juice.

Sauté the almonds in 1 cup butter until lightly browned. Add the grapes and banana slices. Sauté lightly. Pour over the fillets on each plate.

Serve with potatoes, sautéed snow peas and carrots sprinkled with sesame seeds.

Twelve Servings

Whiskey-Seared Salmon with Braised Baby Spinach and Belgian Endive

¾	cup bourbon
½	cup soy sauce
½	cup packed brown sugar
4	(3-ounce) salmon fillets
2	tablespoons chopped shallots
1	tablespoon butter
2	Belgian endives, rinsed
1	pound spinach, rinsed
1½	tablespoons rice wine vinegar
1	tablespoon sugar
	Salt and pepper to taste
3	tablespoons olive oil
¼	cup bourbon
2	tablespoons butter
1	tablespoon lobster roe

❖ ❖ ❖

Mix ¾ cup bourbon, soy sauce and brown sugar in a bowl. Add the salmon. Marinate for 5 minutes.

Sauté the shallots in 1 tablespoon butter in a sauté pan. Add the endives, spinach, vinegar, sugar, salt and pepper and mix gently. Set aside and keep warm.

Remove the salmon from the marinade. Sauté in the olive oil in a nonstick skillet for 2 minutes on each side. Flame with the remaining ¼ cup bourbon. Remove the salmon.

Stir 2 tablespoons butter into the pan drippings. Adjust the seasonings.

Arrange the spinach and endives on plates. Top with the salmon. Pour the sauce over the salmon. Garnish with the lobster roe.

Four Servings

Once, church conventioneers left their rooms so neat and orderly that housekeeping had to disassemble an entire block of rooms to make sure that they were cleaning all that had been used. The staff doesn't always fare so well, however. One time members of a hair-dressers convention had a hair-dying session in a hotel bathtub.

Raspberry Mustard Sauce for Salmon

4	shallots, chopped
1	cup raspberry vinegar
1	cup dry white wine
1	pint raspberries
1	cup fish stock or chicken stock
¼	cup flour
¼	cup butter, softened
½	cup Dijon mustard
¼	cup sugar
	Salt and pepper to taste

❖ ❖ ❖

Cook the shallots in a saucepan over very low heat until translucent. Add the vinegar and wine, stirring to deglaze the skillet. Add 4 tablespoons of the raspberries. Cook until most of the liquid has evaporated. Add the fish stock. Bring to a boil.

Mix the flour and butter into a paste in a cup. Whisk into the shallot mixture gradually. Cook until thickened, stirring frequently.

Add the remaining raspberries, Dijon mustard, sugar, salt and pepper and stir gently. Serve with pan-fried or grilled salmon.

One to Two Cups

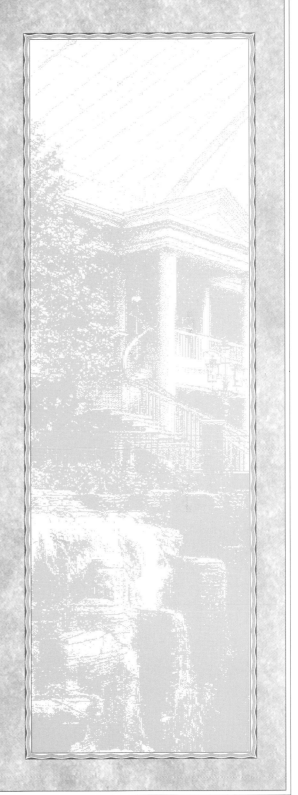

Crab Cakes with Fettuccini and Peppercorn Sauce

Appetizer Crab Cakes are made in the kitchens at Opryland from a recipe that yields 160 portions. The recipe calls for 24 pounds of lump crab meat, 2 pounds of onions, 4 pounds of red and green bell peppers, 4 pounds and 10 ounces of bread crumbs, 12 ounces of garlic, 8 ounces of Creole mustard, 8 ounces of Cajun seasoning, 4 pounds of mayonnaise, 8 ounces of Worcestershire sauce and 7 ounces of fresh lime juice.

Crab Cakes
4   ounces crab leg meat
½   cup bread crumbs
2   tablespoons chopped green or red bell pepper
2   tablespoons chopped onion
1   egg
    Black pepper and cayenne to taste

Peppercorn Sauce
2   tablespoons green peppercorns
3   cups cream
1   tablespoon minced shallots
1   tablespoon minced garlic
    Salt and white pepper to taste
8   ounces crayfish tail meat
2   cups cooked fettuccini or linguini

For the crab cakes, mix the crab meat, bread crumbs, green pepper, onion, egg, salt, black pepper and cayenne in a bowl. Shape into patties. Sauté in a nonstick skillet until golden brown.

For the peppercorn sauce, combine the peppercorns, cream, shallots and garlic in a saucepan. Cook until reduced by ½. Season with salt and white pepper. Add the crayfish meat.

Toss the with the fettuccini. Serve with the crab cakes.

Two Servings

Oyster Velvet

2	tablespoons butter
1	medium onion, chopped
2	ribs celery, chopped
8	ounces shucked oysters
1	tablespoon lemon juice
1	cup white wine
2	cups brandy
¼	cup butter
¼	cup flour
1	(12-ounce) can clam juice
1	cup heavy cream
	Salt and pepper to taste

❖ ❖ ❖

Melt 2 tablespoons butter in a large sauté pan. Add the onion and celery. Sauté until tender. Add the oysters, lemon juice, wine and brandy. Simmer until the oysters are cooked through. Let cool slightly. Purée in a food processor or blender.

Melt ¼ cup butter in a large saucepan. Stir in the flour. Cook for 5 minutes, stirring constantly. Add the clam juice. Cook over low heat until thickened, stirring constantly. Add the oyster mixture and cream. Simmer for 15 minutes. Season with salt and pepper.

Five to Six Servings

Tea-Smoked Shrimp with Saffron Mayonnaise

Shrimp
12	large shrimp, sliced lengthwise
¼	cup dark soy sauce
1	tablespoon sesame oil
	Freshly ground pepper to taste
¼	cup tea leaves
1	tablespoon sugar

Saffron Mayonnaise
2	cloves of garlic, chopped
1	shallot, chopped
	Juice of ½ lemon
	Juice of 1 lime
⅛	teaspoon saffron, or to taste
¼	teaspoon freshly ground pepper
½	teaspoon salt
3	tablespoons balsamic vinaigrette
1	tablespoon chopped parsley
2	tablespoons white wine
2	cups mayonnaise

❖ ❖ ❖

For the shrimp, toss the sliced shrimp with the soy sauce, sesame oil and pepper in a bowl. Fan the shrimp out on a buttered bamboo steamer.

Mix the tea leaves and sugar in a small bowl. Heat over high heat in a dry wok until it begins to smoke. Place the steamer over the wok and cover. Smoke the shrimp until the juices run. Remove from the heat. Let stand for 30 minutes. Return the shrimp to the heat. Steam until the shrimp are cooked through.

For the saffron mayonnaise, combine the garlic, shallot, lemon juice, lime juice, saffron, pepper, salt, balsamic vinaigrette, parsley, wine and mayonnaise in a bowl and mix well. Serve with the shrimp.

One to Two Servings

Shrimp Pasta with Citrus Sauce

Citrus Sauce
 Juice and grated zest of 1 lemon
 Juice and grated zest of 1 lime
 Juice and grated zest of 1 orange
½ cup white vinegar
½ cup white wine
2 tablespoons chopped shallots
½ cup cream
1 cup unsalted butter, cut into cubes
 Salt and white pepper to taste

Shrimp Pasta
24 shrimp
2 tablespoons clarified butter
¼ cup Triple Sec
1 (16-ounce) package pasta, cooked, drained

❖ ❖ ❖

For the sauce, combine the lemon juice, lime juice, orange juice, vinegar, wine and shallots in a saucepan. Cook until the liquid is reduced by ½. Add the cream. Cook until reduced by ½. Remove from the heat.

Whisk in the butter until smooth. Strain through a sieve. Stir in the citrus zest. Season with salt and pepper.

For the shrimp pasta, sauté the shrimp in the butter in a sauté pan or skillet. Add the Triple Sec, stirring to deglaze the skillet. Add the pasta and toss. Stir in the sauce.

Four Servings

The motto of the hotel's superintendent of banquet setup and his staff is "ready for anything." An average day might include events in any or all of five ballrooms, meetings in as many as 85 breakout rooms, exhibits in the 288,000 square feet of exhibit space, banquets, trade shows, the physical displays in the hotel, a golf tournament, a special function at the Wildhorse Saloon in downtown Nashville, and possibly even the grand opening of a new terminal at Nashville's airport.

Eggplant Rolitini

4	thin slices eggplant
2	tablespoons lemon juice
2	cups water
20	ounces shiitake mushrooms, sliced
1	tablespoon butter
	Minced garlic to taste
6	ounces ricotta
	Minced parsley to taste
	Spinach leaves

❖ ❖ ❖

Soak the eggplant in a mixture of the lemon juice and water in a bowl.

Sauté the mushrooms in the butter in a skillet or sauté pan. Remove with a slotted spoon. Add garlic to the skillet. Sauté for several minutes. Remove to a bowl. Add the ricotta cheese and parsley and mix well.

Arrange spinach leaves in four 3-inch squares. Spoon the cheese mixture and mushrooms onto the spinach squares. Roll up as for an envelope; the rolls should resemble small plump logs.

Drain the eggplant and press to remove water. Place 1 mushroom log on each eggplant slice and roll up, tucking in the sides.

Grill until the eggplant is cooked through.

Two Servings

Louisiana Red Lentils and Roasted Corn Ragout

1	(16-ounce) package dried red lentils
¼	cup minced garlic
1½	cups finely chopped onions
2	tablespoons white vinegar
½	(20-ounce) package frozen corn, thawed, roasted
1	bunch scallions, finely chopped
½	cup finely chopped green bell pepper
½	cup finely chopped red bell pepper
	Juice of ½ to 1 lime
¼	cup chopped parsley
¼	cup chopped chives
¾	cup Roma tomatoes
	Salt, black pepper and cayenne to taste

❖ ❖ ❖

Sort and rinse the lentils. Sauté the garlic and onions in a large heavy nonstick saucepan until translucent. Add the lentils. Sauté for 2 minutes. Add the vinegar and mix well.

Add enough water to cover. Cook over medium heat until the water is absorbed. Remove from the heat.

Add the corn, scallions, green pepper and red pepper and mix well. Stir in the lime juice, parsley, chives and tomatoes gently. Season with the salt, black pepper and cayenne. Cook until heated through.

Six to Eight Servings

For delicious Steamed Vegetables like those served at Opryland, select fresh vegetables such as carrots, cauliflower, broccoli, and zucchini. Place over, but not in, salted water. Add a bay leaf, thyme, or other herb of choice. Steam for ten minutes or until done to taste. Season with lemon juice, butter, salt, and pepper.

Creamed Spinach

2½	pounds spinach, rinsed, drained, patted dry
1	medium onion, finely chopped
	Olive oil
2	tablespoons Pernod
½	cup heavy cream
	Salt and pepper to taste

❖ ❖ ❖

Sauté the spinach and onion in olive oil in a sauté pan just until tender-crisp. Add the Pernod. Cook until tender. Drain in a colander.

Bring the cream to a simmer in a large saucepan. Simmer until reduced by ⅔. Add the spinach gradually. Cook until heated through, stirring frequently. Season with salt and pepper.

Four to Six Servings

Fettuccini Alfredo

1	(16-ounce) package fettuccini
	Salt to taste
2	teaspoons butter
6	ounces prosciutto, julienned
1	tablespoon minced onion
½	cup white wine
1	quart heavy cream
½	cup freshly grated Parmesan cheese
	Salt and pepper to taste

❖ ❖ ❖

Cook the fettuccini in boiling salted water in a stockpot until tender; drain well. Stir in 1 teaspoon of the butter. Set aside and keep warm.

Melt the remaining 1 teaspoon butter in a 9-inch skillet. Add the ham and onion. Cook until the onion is translucent. Add the wine and cream. Cook until reduced by ½. Stir in the cheese. Season with salt and pepper.

Toss the pasta with the sauce in a serving bowl, coating well.

Four to Six Servings

Poppy Seed and Oat Rolls

1	envelope dry yeast
2½	cups lukewarm (68- to 72-degree) water
1	cup cracked oats
3	tablespoons poppy seeds
2	tablespoons shortening
2	tablespoons honey
1	teaspoon salt
4½	cups flour

❖ ❖ ❖

Dissolve the yeast in the lukewarm water. Combine with the oats, poppy seeds, shortening, honey, salt and flour in a mixer bowl. Mix with a dough hook for 10 to 12 minutes or until a soft dough forms.

Place the dough in a greased bowl, turning to coat the surface. Let rise, covered, in a warm place for 1 hour. Punch the dough down. Let rise, covered, for 30 minutes.

Shape into rolls. Place on greased baking sheets. Let rise until doubled in bulk.

Bake at 400 degrees for 12 to 15 minutes or until golden brown.

One Dozen

Opryland Hotel's pastry chef created a four-square-foot chocolate sculpture that won first place in Nashville's annual Incredible Edible Chocolate Festival. The 10-pound "Treasure Island" delight of semisweet and white chocolate featured palm trees, a cockatoo, and a treasure chest filled with chocolate, and required 120 hours to complete. The hotel's chef garde manger placed second in the competition with his 50-pound semisweet chocolate castle.

Bananas Foster

1	cup butter
2	cups packed brown sugar
	Juice of 2 oranges
1	teaspoon cinnamon
2	bananas, sliced
	Vanilla ice cream

❖ ❖ ❖

Melt the butter in a sauté pan or skillet. Add the brown sugar. Cook until the brown sugar is dissolved, stirring constantly. Add the orange juice, cinnamon and bananas. Sauté until lightly browned.

Spoon over the ice cream in dessert dishes to serve.

Two Servings

Crème Anglaise

3   cups milk
½   cup sugar
1   tablespoon vanilla extract
12   egg yolks, slightly beaten
1   tablespoon cinnamon

❖ ❖ ❖

Combine the milk, sugar and vanilla in a saucepan and mix
gently. Cook until the mixture registers 115 degrees, stirring
frequently. Stir a small amount of the hot mixture into the egg
yolks; stir the egg yolks into the hot mixture.

Cook until the mixture coats the back of a spoon, stirring
constantly; do not overcook to avoid scrambling the eggs.
Remove from the heat. Stir in the cinnamon. Pour into a bowl
or dessert dishes. Chill thoroughly.

Four Servings

Chocolate Concorde

Meringue
1   (1-pound) package confectioners' sugar
1   cup baking cocoa
16 egg whites
2   cups sugar

Mousse
13 egg whites
¼   cup sugar
1   pound chocolate
1   cup butter, softened
2   egg yolks

Cake
3   baked (10-inch) chocolate cake layers

❖ ❖ ❖

For the meringue, sift the confectioners' sugar and cocoa together. Beat the egg whites and ¼ of the sugar in a bowl with a balloon whisk until soft peaks form, beginning at low speed and increasing speed gradually. Add the remaining sugar gradually, beating until stiff peaks form and the sugar is dissolved. Fold in the cocoa mixture. Spoon carefully into a pastry bag fitted with a number-14 nozzle. Pipe in a spiral into three 9-inch circles on the parchment-lined baking sheet. Pipe the remaining meringue into straight lines. Bake at 300 degrees for 40 to 45 minutes or until lightly browned; cool.

For the mousse, beat the egg whites with the sugar in a mixer bowl until stiff peaks form. Melt the chocolate in a double boiler over simmering water. Place the butter in a bowl. Add the melted chocolate and egg yolks alternately, mixing well. Fold in the beaten egg whites.

To assemble, place 1 meringue circle over each cake layer. Spread each circle with some of the mousse. Stack the cake layers. Spread the remaining mousse over the side of the cake to cover. Chill for 10 minutes or until set. Cut the straight pieces of meringue into 1½-inch pieces. Arrange over the cake.

Twelve to Sixteen Servings

In the far corner of the pastry kitchen, there is a little-noticed locked door that leads to a small room that contains the wonderful aroma of chocolate. The room, like a walk-in safe, contains an incredible collection of chocolate sculpture, with everything from a model of a Jaguar hood ornament to a soaring chocolate eagle with a 7-foot wing span that required a mere 120 hours to sculpt. At the other end of the spectrum are chocolate boxes, swans, and roses. One of the pastry chef's favorite projects was a 6-foot bunny, "but he's no longer around."

There are two ways to produce a chocolate sculpture. It can be chiseled from a block of chocolate, or soft chocolate can be sculpted with the hands. The chef starts with a block of chocolate that ranges from 10 to 40 pounds, depending on the size of the intended sculpture. He uses a paring knife and several ceramic carving tools to chisel. After each work session, the partially finished sculpture is refrigerated. A sculpture may require between 30 and 150 hours to complete.

Gâteau d'Orleans

Sugar Syrup
1   cup sugar
1   cup water
Ganache
2   pounds milk chocolate
1   pound semisweet chocolate
5   cups heavy cream
1   tablespoon sugar, or to taste
Chocolate Cake (page 187)

For the sugar syrup, boil 1 cup sugar and water in a saucepan until syrupy. Set aside.

For the ganache, heat the milk chocolate and semisweet chocolate in a double boiler over hot water until the chocolate begins to melt. Add 4 cups of the cream. Cook until the chocolate is melted, stirring frequently. Cool to lukewarm.

Beat the remaining 1 cup cream in a mixer bowl until soft peaks form. Add 1 tablespoon sugar gradually, beating constantly until the sugar is dissolved and stiff peaks form.

Sprinkle each cake layer with a small amount of the sugar syrup. Place 1 cake layer on a serving plate and spread with some of the ganache. Top with a second layer and spread with some of the ganache. Spread the third layer with the whipped cream; spread the fourth layer with some of the ganache. Spread the fifth layer and the side of all layers with the remaining ganache or melt the remaining ganache and pour over the layers.

Twelve Servings

Chocolate Cake

5	cups cake flour
2⅔	cups sugar
8	teaspoons baking powder
1	tablespoon baking soda
1⅓	cups baking cocoa
12½	to 13 tablespoons butter, softened
13	to 14 tablespoons melted shortening
2¼	cups milk
4	eggs

❖　❖　❖

Combine the flour, sugar, baking powder, baking soda and cocoa in a mixer bowl and beat well. Add the butter and shortening. Beat for 5 to 7 minutes or until well blended. Add the milk and eggs. Beat until mixed, scraping the bowl frequently.

Pour into 5 greased and floured round cake pans. Bake at 350 degrees for 30 minutes or until the layers test done. Cool in the pans for several minutes. Remove to a wire rack to cool completely.

Twelve Servings

Rice Pudding with Raspberry Sauce

Rice Pudding
1   gallon milk
9   ounces rice
1   cup sugar
8   ounces golden raisins
1   teaspoon vanilla extract
Raspberry Sauce
¼   cup water
¼   cup confectioners' sugar
2   cups raspberries
¼   cup brandy
2   tablespoons cornstarch

❖ ❖ ❖

For the pudding, bring the milk to a boil in a saucepan. Add the rice. Cook until tender. Add the sugar, raisins and vanilla and mix gently. Let cool.

For the sauce, bring the water, confectioners' sugar and raspberries to a boil in a saucepan. Add the brandy. Simmer for 5 minutes. Mix the cornstarch with a small amount of cold water. Stir quickly into the hot sauce. Cook until thickened, stirring constantly.

Spoon the pudding into dessert glasses. Spoon the sauce over the top.

Sixteen Servings

Fresh Apple Pie

1	cup cake crumbs
1	unbaked (9-inch) pie shell
4	or 5 medium apples, peeled, sliced
2	eggs
2	tablespoons sugar
6	tablespoons milk
2	tablespoons heavy cream
	Salt and vanilla extract to taste

❖ ❖ ❖

Sprinkle the cake crumbs in the pie shell. Arrange the sliced apples over the cake crumbs.

Combine the eggs and sugar in a bowl and mix well. Add the milk, cream, salt and vanilla and mix well. Pour over the apples.

Bake at 350 degrees for 45 to 50 minutes or until the filling is set and the crust is golden brown. Cool on a wire rack.

Six to Eight Servings

Tiny Pecan Pies

3	ounces cream cheese, softened
½	cup butter or margarine, softened
1	cup sifted flour
⅔	cup coarsely broken pecans
1	egg
¾	cup packed brown sugar
1	tablespoon butter or margarine, softened
1	teaspoon vanilla extract
	Salt to taste

❖ ❖ ❖

Combine the cream cheese and ½ cup butter in a bowl and blend well. Add the flour and mix until smooth. Chill for 1 hour.

Shape into 24 small balls. Press over the bottom and side of ungreased 1¾-inch muffin cups or tart shells.

Sprinkle half the pecans into the prepared muffin cups.

Combine the egg, brown sugar, 1 tablespoon butter, vanilla and salt in a mixer bowl and mix well. Spoon over the pecans in the muffin cups. Sprinkle with the remaining pecans.

Bake at 325 degrees for 25 minutes or until set. Cool in the muffin cups.

Twenty-Four Servings

Index

Order Form

For additional copies of *A Taste of Tradition*, we are providing this easy order form for your convenience. For your own enjoyment, or for gift giving, you might wish to consider adding one of our very popular food products to your order.

Item Description	Qty.	Cost	Extension
A Taste of Tradition Cookbook	____	$ 19.95	_____
Opryland Hotel *Delta Dill Dressing*	____	5.99	_____
Opryland Hotel *Opry Onion Relish*	____	5.99	_____
Opryland Hotel *Volunteer Kick Salsa*	____	5.99	_____
Opryland Hotel *Minnie Pearl Peppercorn Dressing*	____	5.99	_____
Opryland Hotel *Tennessee Pepper Sauce*	____	5.99	_____
Opryland Hotel *Magnolia Marinade*	____	5.99	_____
Opryland Hotel *Jackson Blackberry Jam*	____	5.99	_____
Opryland Hotel *Southern Peach Delight*	____	5.99	_____
Opryland Hotel *Nashville's Best BBQ*	____	5.99	_____
Add Shipping			$ 5.00
Total			_____

Ship to: _____

_____

_____

Phone: _____

Credit Card Charge: Card: _____ No. _____

Expiration Date: _____ Name on Card: _____

Mail Form to: Opryland Hotel Bushels & Baskets Shoppe
2800 Opryland Drive
Nashville, Tennessee 37214
615/889-1000 extension 48131
615/871-6789 FAX

Please feel free to photocopy this page to use in ordering books and gifts.